Services for Children in Need:
From Policy to Practice

STROUD COLLEGE LIBRARY

TWO WEEK LOANS

WITHDRAWN

D1352823

T25020

Studies in Evaluating the Children Act 1989

Series editors:
Dr Carolyn Davies, Prof. Jane Aldgate

Other titles in the series include
From Care to Accommodation
Parental Perspectives on Care Proceedings
The Last Resort
Leaving Care in Partnership
Safeguarding Children with the Children Act 1989
The Best-Laid Plans
Supporting Families through Short-term Fostering
Expert Evidence in Child Protection Litigation
Family Support in Cases of Emotional Maltreatment and Neglect
Fostering Family Contact
The Children Act Now

STUDIES IN EVALUATING THE CHILDREN ACT 1989

Services for Children in Need: From Policy to Practice

Jane Tunstill
Royal Holloway, University of London

Jane Aldgate
The Open University

London: The Stationery Office

362.7 (2wk)

T25020

STROUD COLLEGE
LIBRARY

© Crown copyright 2000. Published with the permission of the Department of Health on behalf of the Controller of Her Majesty's Stationery Office.

All rights reserved.

Copyright in the typographical arrangement and design is invested in The Stationery Office Limited. Applications for reproduction should be made in writing in the first instance to The Copyright Unit, Her Majesty's Stationery Office, St Clements House, 2–16 Colegate, Norwich NR3 1BQ.

First published 2000

ISBN 0 11 322442 7

Published by The Stationery Office and available from:

The Publications Centre
(mail, telephone and fax orders only)
PO Box 276, London SW8 5DT
Telephone orders/enquiries 0870 600 5522
Fax orders 0870 600 5533

www.thestationeryoffice.com

The Stationery Office Bookshops
123 Kingsway, London WC2B 6PQ
020 7242 6393 Fax 020 7242 6394
68–69 Bull Street, Birmingham B4 6AD
0121 236 9696 Fax 0121 236 9699
33 Wine Street, Bristol BS1 2BQ
0117 926 4306 Fax 0117 929 4515
9–21 Princess Street, Manchester M60 8AS
0161 834 7201 Fax 0161 833 0634
16 Arthur Street, Belfast BT1 4GD
028 9023 8451 Fax 028 9023 5401
The Stationery Office Oriel Bookshop
18–19 High Street, Cardiff CF1 2BZ
029 2039 5548 Fax 029 2038 4347
71 Lothian Road, Edinburgh EH3 9AZ
0870 606 5566 Fax 0870 606 5588

The Stationery Office's Accredited Agents
(see Yellow Pages)

and through good booksellers

Printed in the United Kingdom for The Stationery Office
TJ002767 10/00 C10 9385 13703

For Pauline Hardiker with our gratitude for her inspiration and scholarship

Contents

Figures and tables

Figures

Tables

Foreword

The Children Act 1989 was implemented on 14 October 1991. At its launch the then Lord Chancellor, Lord Mackay, described the Act as 'the most radical legislative reform to children's services this century'. Shortly after the launch the Department of Health put together a strategy to monitor and evaluate the initial impact of the Act. Taking a tripartite approach, this drew on evidence from statistical returns, inspections and research to develop a rounded appreciation of early implementation. The subsequent strategy plan was published and circulated to relevant bodies, including social services and the major voluntary agencies, in 1993. This plan formed the backcloth for a programme of research studies commissioned by the Department of Health to explore early evaluation in more depth. It is these studies, some 20 in all, which form this new series.

The programme studies investigate the implementation of key changes introduced by the Act and evaluate the facilitators and inhibitors to the meeting of key objectives. A longer term goal of the programme is to review the aims of the Act in the light of implementation with a view to reconsideration or amendment should this be felt necessary. Finally, a more general and important scientific aim is to consider how far change could be achieved successfully by changing the law.

There are several principles underlying the Children Act 1989 that permeate the research studies. An important strand of the Act is to bring together private and public law so that the needs of all children whose welfare is at risk might be approached in the same way. This philosophy is underpinned by the principle of promoting children's welfare. There should be recognition of children's time-scales and, in court cases, children's welfare should be paramount. To aid this paramountcy principle there should be a welfare checklist, and delays in court hearings should be avoided.

The promotion of children's welfare takes a child development focus, urging local authorities to take a holistic and corporate approach to providing services. Departments such as health, education, housing, police, social services and recreation should work together to respond to children's needs. Children, the Act argues, are best looked after within their families wherever possible and, where not, the continuing support of parents and wider kin should be facilitated by avoiding compulsory proceedings whenever possible. Parents should be partners in any intervention process, and children's views should be sought and listened to in any decision-making affecting their lives. To promote continuity for children looked after, contact with families should be encouraged and children's religion, culture, ethnicity and language should be preserved.

Local authorities have a duty to move from services to prevent care to a broader remit of providing family support, which could include planned periods away from home. However, family support services should not be universal but target those most in need. The introduction of Children's Services Plans in 1996 has made the idea of corporate responsibility a more tangible reality and seeks to help local authorities look at how they may use scarce resources cost-effectively.

The themes of the Children Act have relevance for the millennium. The concern with combating social exclusion is echoed through several of the studies, especially those on family support and young people looked after by local authorities. The value of early intervention is also a theme in the studies on family centres, day care and services for children defined as 'in need' under the Act. Further, the research on the implementation of the Looking After Children Schedules emphasises the importance to children in foster and residential care of attaining good outcomes in education. Lastly, attending to the health of parents and their children is another strand in both the family support and 'children looked after' studies.

To accompany the 20 individual studies in the research programme the Department of Health has commissioned an overview of the findings, to be published by The Stationery Office in the style of similar previous publications from HMSO: *Social Work Decisions in Child Care 1985*; *Patterns and Outcomes in Child Care 1991*; *Child Protection: Messages from Research 1996*; and *Focus on Teenagers 1997*.

The editors would like to express their appreciation to the members of the research community; professionals from different disciplines, and service users, among others, who have contributed so willingly and generously to the successful completion of the research studies and to the construction of the overview. Without their help, none of the research would have been written or disseminated.

Carolyn Davies
Jane Aldgate

Acknowledgements

We would like to record our special gratitude for the commitment, ability, hard work and patience of Marilyn Hughes, without whom this study would not have been completed. We would also like to thank other members of the research team who made a valuable contribution to design and data collection: Marie Bradley, Pam Freeman, David Hawley and Angela Spriggs.

We are also indebted to Dr Carolyn Davies at the Department of Health for encouragement and support of our endeavours and to academic colleagues in our own and other universities, in particular: Dr Dorothy Atkinson, Professor Mike Bury, Hedy Cleaver, Rupert Hughes, Dr Linda Jones, Professor Francis Robinson, Wendy Rose and Professor June Thoburn.

A special tribute goes to the administrative help received from our universities over the period of study: Julie Stock at The Open University; Christine Cazalet at Leicester University; Sheila Sweet, Liz Hudson and Shirley Chambers at Royal Holloway College, University of London. Their expertise and their endurance of our many drafts led to a finished product that was a publication in its own right. Their courtesy and generosity in dealings with our academic colleagues was also much appreciated.

Senior colleagues in the social services departments involved in the study have been extremely generous with their advice and support. We thank them all, and especially Steven Barber, Felicity Budgen, Terry Earland, Jane Held, Margie Rooke, Jane Streather, Paul Sutton and Steve Walker.

Finally, we would like to thank our seven participating authorities for their co-operation and enthusiasm. We owe much to the children and families who gave us their time and their illuminating views on the services they had received. We hope that these views will be useful to the seven authorities and to many other professionals who strive to improve family support services for children in need and their families.

Jane Tunstill
Jane Aldgate

1 Introduction and background to the study

The subject of this book, family support, is a recurrent topic in current political, professional and public debates about child-care social work. Its apparent simplicity belies the potential breadth of the tasks involved, and the consequent challenges, in attempting to evaluate its impact. For example, as the Audit Commission has argued: 'Family support can include any activity or facility provided either by statutory agencies or by community groups or individuals, aimed at providing advice and support to parents to help them in bringing up their children.' (Audit Commission 1994, p. 82) The challenges of implementing family support services have also been recognised as considerable: 'Part III of the Act is the most difficult to implement. But if the Children Act is to be a success, it is the part to which most sustained attention must be given.' (Freeman 1992, p. 49)

In other words, the intrinsic complexity of the concept of family support has to be the starting point for any serious understanding of the effectiveness of wider Children Act implementation strategies. Therefore, the starting point for this book is an overview of the concept of children in need with reference to theory, policy and practice. This has three areas:

- ◆ the evolution of the concept of children in need;
- ◆ the policy and legislative framework for children in need; and
- ◆ the wider policy framework.

The evolution of the concept of children in need

Within the space of three decades, three major child-care Acts have been placed on the statute books in England and Wales:

- ◆ the Children and Young Persons' Act 1963;
- ◆ the Children Act 1975; and
- ◆ the Children Act 1989.

Each Act enshrines very different models of the requisite relationship between state, family and child, and reflects the respective political and social era in which it was passed. In the context of policies towards children in their own homes and of the relationships that they experience with members of their own families and wider communities, the main conceptual, theoretical and legal shifts have been from protection to prevention through family support to children in need.

Prevention

The concept of prevention has the longest pedigree of various approaches to working with children in their families, with most commentators dating its birth to 1948 (Holman 1988; Parker 1990). Whilst the Children Act 1948 omitted to mention 'prevention', it seems that the absence of a duty to prevent negative outcomes, including reception into care, stimulated child-care workers into a range of preventive activity which was finally officially recognised and consolidated within Section 1 of the Children and Young Persons' Act 1963.

However, the consensus around *what was to be prevented* rapidly broke down (Parker 1990). Packman (1975) records that, in spite of a brief consensus around the desirability of preventing reception into care, it began to be perceived that there were issues in the home lives of the children in question, such as the nature of their parenting experiences, which also needed addressing. Even here, differing solutions found favour. Some practitioners focused exclusively on a psycho-dynamic model of casework. Others placed more emphasis on structural factors and acknowledged the complementary value of providing services such as day care and, indeed, financial assistance. Yet others combined different approaches under the umbrella of psycho-social.

The shift towards child rescue and protection

The Children Act 1975 altered the balance between the family and the state in placing an emphasis on children's time-scales and making it possible to sever parental rights on grounds of time rather than parental incapacity. Permanency planning for children to be with alternative families became fashionable at the beginning of the 1980s. This approach was fuelled by the death in the early 1970s of Maria Colwell, who had been returned from care to her family and died at the hands of her stepfather. The growing emphasis on detection of child abuse from the early 1980s onwards also took the emphasis away from prevention.

The move towards family support

By the middle of the 1980s, anxieties about the imbalance between supporting and removing children had led to a rebalancing of intervention with a move back towards trying to keep children with their own families. This change was encouraged by research that expressed growing concerns about the quality of state care as an alternative to preventive strategies in the community (see Department of Health and Social Security 1985).

Packman's work was of special significance in this period in that she identified the tendency of social workers to reduce prevention to a strict gatekeeping role by providing care for children without offering alternative help (Packman 1986). Her work underlined the need for a wider perspective, including avoiding a problem-focused approach and looking at the potential role of the extended as well as the nuclear family, in order to produce better assessments and a broader range of solutions for family problems. The political values of the period were receptive to these messages and combined to refocus social policy on the positive value of the family and, in the various documents that led to the Children Act 1989, to suggest the value of a wider concept of family support.

Existing research data provide no specific pointers as to the operational limits of family support but underline the value of offering resources to the child in the family, in the community. Gibbons (1990) is an exception in that she explicitly links family support and prevention. She concluded that broad-based family support could be achieved through independent family and child-care projects.

Family support: an evolving concept

As many writers point out, family support has evolved in the broader context of policy towards children. Given that this whole policy area is intimately connected to political, professional and empirical values, social constructions of family support will inevitably change considerably over time. This evolutionary tendency underlines the importance of research data that will permit accurate judgements to be made about both the effectiveness of current approaches and the appropriateness of emerging trends in policy and practice. Indeed, currently, debates about family support policies have started to emphasise specifically the concept of 'parenting'. This is apparent in current government activity: for example, in the consultation paper on supporting families (Home Office 1998), which includes an outline of the recently established National Family and Parenting Institute and in the parenting orders in the Criminal Justice Act 1997. The Sure Start initiative is intended to facilitate and support the development of the satisfactory parenting behaviour of parents in socio-economically deprived areas (Glass 1999, pp. 257–64).

The policy and legislative framework for children in need

The Children Act 1989 was passed in the context of a wider policy framework and with an emphasis on co-operation and collaborative activity. The importance of the Children Act 1989 is that it has consolidated and, in some cases, recast the duties and responsibilities of earlier child-care legislation in the following threefold way:

- ♦ from a broad assumption of practice emanating from social work advice and counselling to a wider remit of service delivery;

- ♦ from the relatively narrow concept of 'prevention' of reception into care to the broader concept of family support and promotion of welfare; and

- ♦ from a concern about an undifferentiated group of children to a specific group who are defined as 'children in need'.

It marks a radical change in approach to family support which has been summarised by Rose:

> The Children Act places a duty on local authorities to safeguard and promote the welfare of children in their area who are in need and, subject to that duty, to promote the upbringing of such children by their families. The new emphasis in Section 17 is for the local authorities to work with or facilitate the work of others.
>
> This is reinforced in Section 27, with the new duty on other agencies to assist local authorities to influence others in the way they work with families (partnership in all aspects) and to encourage multidisciplinary working and mutual understanding between all agencies.
>
> The new provisions of the Children Act enable a range of services such as accommodation not to be seen as a breakdown in preventive service but as a positive measure of family support. They allow for the development of imaginative and flexible services in partnership and in support of families, with the users' views fully taken into account and services assessed against the welfare checklist of Section 1. Such developments have a relatively recent history. (Rose 1992, p. ix)

Section 17(10) of the Children Act 1989 states that a child is 'in need' if:

(a) he is unlikely to achieve or maintain, or to have the opportunity of achieving or maintaining, a reasonable standard of health or development without the provision for him of services by a local authority;

(b) his health or development is likely to be significantly impaired, or further impaired, without the provision for him of such services; or

(c) he is disabled.

Section 11 specifies that:

♦ 'development' means physical, intellectual, emotional, social or behavioural development; and

♦ 'health' means physical or mental health.

As well as outlining the broad policy areas that fall within the scope of the 'in need' definition, Section 27 states how this work should be achieved, i.e., through co-operation between the social services department, defined in the Act as the 'local authority', and other organisations:

(1) Where it appears to a local authority that any authority or other person mentioned in sub-section (3) could, by taking any specified action, help in the exercise of any of their functions under this part, they may request the help of that other authority or person, specifying the action in question.

(2) An authority whose help is so requested shall comply with the request if it is compatible with their own statutory or other duties and obligations and it does not unduly prejudice the discharge of any of their functions.

(3) The persons are:
(a) any local authority;
(b) any education authority;
(c) any local housing authority;
(d) any health authority; and
(e) any person authorised by the Secretary of State for the purposes of this section.

(4) Every local authority shall assist any local education authority with the provision of services for any child within the local authority's area who has special educational needs.

Additionally, Section 17(5) concerns the facilitation of service provision via organisations other than the local authority (i.e., social services departments), including voluntary and private organisations.

The wider policy framework

The Children Act 1989 has been only one of several recent legislative changes of central importance to the work of statutory agencies in local government. Other major events have been the implementation of the National Health Service and Community Care Act 1990, which has required local authorities (defined in its usual sense, outside that of the Children Act 1989) for the first time to produce an annual plan of the services for the community, in consultation with local health authorities and National Health Service trusts.

The Education Act 1981 has set out the requirements for the assessment and 'statementing' of children with disabilities and other special educational needs, whilst the Education Reform Act 1988 set out details of the National Curriculum and also required that local authorities publish 'league tables' derived from a variety of information about individual schools, such as public examination results, records of attendance and suspensions and exclusions from schools.

In addition, the Criminal Justice Act 1991 established the Youth Courts for 10–17-year-olds, continuing the practice of social workers in social service departments having the responsibility for preparation of court reports. It introduced the power for magistrates to require parents to attend court, the payment of fines by parents or other guardians and new powers to bind over parents or guardians. Where an offender is under 16 years of age, the binding over of the parents/guardians is a duty the court uses when it believes this would be desirable in the interests of preventing further offences.

These new powers are based on the concept of parental responsibility, and to some extent, though with significant differences, they echo the concept of parental responsibility in the Children Act 1989.

Since 1997, and the election of the new Labour government, a range of new policy initiatives has been introduced, both in the context of existing legislation and as a response to perceived flaws and deficits of such legislation. However, the point must be made that the study reported here was commissioned before most of these new developments came on stream.

Whilst it is too early to take any meaningful account of the impact of initiatives such as the National Childcare Strategy, Quality Protects and Sure Start, this study – along with others in the Children Act research series (particularly Aldgate and Tunstill 1995; Aldgate and Bradley 1999; Thoburn et al. 2000; DoH 2000a) – provides cumulative research evidence that early intervention to support children and families is essential before problems become so severe that they place children at risk of significant harm.

The emphasis on co-operation and collaborative activity

A consistent and important strand in all these recent developments is the value of co-operation both between local authority departments and between local authorities and other agencies, especially health and education authorities and trusts and voluntary organisations. Evidence in the first national study of the implementation of Section 17 (Aldgate and Tunstill 1995) suggests that, in spite of variations in local interpretations of children 'in need', a high proportion of social services departments actually consulted other organisations, either via meetings or by sharing policy documents, in order to plan their original implementation strategies.

Work by the Social Services Inspectorate (Hickman and Barnes 1993) also suggests that Children's Services Plans have involved collaboration between the departments of social services, education, housing and health, the probation service, the police and voluntary organisations.

In addition to consultation, co-operation ought to involve work at the strategic level, including, for example, joint planning, joint purchase of services, co-operation in relation to specific issues such as truancy and school exclusion, or the provision of specialist services for children with both emotional and health needs.

Smith and Grimshaw (1989), however, predicted that the traditional boundaries between education and social services concerning work with truancy and school refusers would need to shift, providing new possibilities for collaborative work as well as adding to workload stresses, with the responsibility for court proceedings shifting to the Education Welfare Service.

Strategic work both within local authorities and between them and other agencies may have a direct bearing on the range and effectiveness of services available, in particular family support services. Aldgate and Tunstill (1995) point to a pattern of social services departments retaining control of services, such as the provision of accommodation and investigative work, but forming new partnerships with education and leisure and the voluntary sector in relation to other work, for example, after-school provision or family centres.

Interagency work may be seen as operating on at least two levels, the co-operative practice between professionals and collaboration at the policy and management level. The evidence for the success of interagency collaboration at a strategic level is mixed. It is clear that the presence of strategic inter-agency work could have an affect on both the planning task and on day-to-day inter-professional work.

Aldgate and Tunstill (1995) and Hickman and Barnes (1993) both suggest that, in general, social services departments consult several agencies in the process of planning their work. Hickman and Barnes suggest that 70% of authorities who had either completed (or were in the process of completing) Children's Services Plans, had collaborated with Education in the formulation of these plans.

In contrast, Robbins (1990) found that, although social services departments did include interagency issues in their policy documents, in general they were not given a high profile. For example, only a small number of authorities included routine collaboration concerning truancy within their policy documents, and there did not seem to have been a strong focus on interagency decision-making.

Some issues in co-operative practice

Interagency work is not new and has been part of the post-war welfare arrangements in social work, health and education for several decades. The Children and Young Persons' Act 1969, for example, included a clause whereby failure to attend school could be grounds for care proceedings. These cases necessitated collaborative activity between the departments of social services and education.

Such activity is not without problems. In their extensive review of disruption in schools, Skinner et al. (1983) pointed out that the police and probation officers tended to be viewed favourably by staff in schools. In contrast, social workers were viewed unfavourably, in part because of their style of work, which was seen as tending to focus on the particular circumstances of the family and child rather than on, for example, absenteeism.

This report also suggested that social workers were seen as being poor at communication with schools and were criticised for being too busy to respond. In addition, the relatively inflexible timetables of education staff did not facilitate good communication: at the primary level, break-times often provided the only potential opportunities for contact with other workers.

Some of the problems may be accounted for by the emphasis given to certain aspects of their work by social workers. Skinner et al. (1983) have pointed out that much of the social services work with children of primary school age is concerned with child protection issues, rather than with the broader concerns of pupil behaviour at school, so that the policies and practices relating to child protection may influence all other work.

There may also be difficulties associated with traditional values and boundaries within different agencies. Robbins (1993) reported on research involving a sample of Community Mental Handicap Teams, with staff from the departments of health, social services and education working together to meet the needs of people with learning difficulties. Although staff did not experience the difficulty of being located on different sites, the study found that staff still operated within their 'traditional' boundaries, in part because the agencies that provided the 'base' for their work had not shifted their perspectives or management style.

There can be positive developments. Work by Gibbons (1990) suggested that social services' staff who were 'out-posted' into community-based services could begin to work in different ways from the 'parent' agency.

Collaboration can work at many levels, and examples of positive approaches are illustrated by, for example, Lloyd (1993), in a Rowntree-funded project that focuses on interagency work in practice, aimed at the adolescent age group. Similarly, Aldgate and Bradley (1999) provide practice examples of close collaboration between social workers and health visitors in the provision of respite care for families under stress.

It can be seen, therefore, that the context of interagency connections and the legislative framework for providing family support services are both necessary aspects of the infrastructure to provide professional services to families and their children who are defined as 'in need'.

Key issues from research into family support within the Children Act 1989

By the time that the present study was initiated, the Department of Health had, within the Children Act research programme, already commissioned several studies relating to the implementation of family support arrangements (see DoH 2000a), and it is helpful to set the study reported here alongside the other Children Act studies.

When this study began, work had already been done on the use of family centres and day care for the under-fives (see DoH 2000a). Work by Statham (1994) and Candapa et al. (1995) on day-care services have added to the body of knowledge on children under 8 years. The work of Petrie et al. (1992) on out-of-school schemes describes the broader remit of family support services to support working parents, while the study of short-term fostering illustrates the augmentation of family support to include the use of accommodation under Section 20 as a service to prevent family breakdown (Aldgate and Bradley 1999).

In the sphere of child maltreatment, the work of Brandon and colleagues (1999) on children at risk of significant harm pointed to the importance of moving from identification of risk to identification of the impact of harm on children and to the services to counteract that harm. Similarly, Thoburn et al. (2000) draw attention to the value of family support services in cases of child neglect.

The role of the voluntary sector in family support services within the Children Act was addressed by Tunstill and Ozolins (1994), whilst Stace and Tunstill (1990) looked at the potential conflicts between the Children Act 1989 and the NHS Community Care Act 1991.

Finally, the Social Services Inspectorate (1992) had examined the implementation of Section 17 in London and, using a survey method across policy-makers and managers, Aldgate and Tunstill (1995) provided an overview of the tasks undertaken to ascertain the extent of need, to establish priorities in access to services and to develop services and plan the future development of services across England. Colton et al. (1993) had similarly investigated the implementation of Section 17 in Wales.

There were striking similarities between the picture of implementation emerging in the studies of London boroughs and nationally in England, with a particular overlap in the emergence of a hierarchy of access to services, based on a distinction between two groups of children: those 'in the community' and children 'for whom local authorities already had some responsibility' (Aldgate and Tunstill 1995).

The Aldgate and Tunstill study (1995) identified some key factors in the implementation process. Staff in several of the social services departments visited expressed the view that a disproportionate amount of attention was paid to under-fives in comparison with children aged between 7–12 and over 15.

Two key issues emerged, with implications across the continuum of family support for children in need:

- ◆ The nature of statutory responsibility had been misunderstood: 'statutory responsibility' tended to be seen as synonymous with child protection investigation.

- ◆ Implementation of Section 17, contrary to the intentions of the Act, had taken the form of 'service-led' rather than 'needs-led' policies.

There were important, if unavoidable, gaps in the information provided by both the London and the national studies. None of the studies was intended to provide more than a snapshot of the situation at one point in time, nor to give information about the experiences of individual children and their families, either at a fixed point in time or in the period following the first request for, or experience of access to, services. Perhaps most pressing, in the light of the philosophy of the Act, was the need for information on users' perceptions of services.

The work reviewed underlined the gaps in knowledge about service provision and delivery for children in need. It was with these issues in mind that this study of children in need was planned. Its aim was to monitor and evaluate the provision, and, to some extent, the delivery, of family support services to a group of children in need in seven local authorities.

2 *Aims and objectives of the study*

From the work outlined in Chapter 1 we formulated the following overall research aim:

> to monitor and evaluate the provision and, to some extent, the delivery of family support services to a group of children in need and to their immediate and extended families.

Within this aim, there were a number of specific objectives:

♦ to identify the characteristics of those children and families referred to Social Services, excluding formal child protection enquires and disability referrals;

♦ to contrast and compare the characteristics of children and families who received services with those who did not;

♦ to investigate the impact of the delivery of services provided on individual children, their parents and their wider families;

♦ to describe and investigate the provision of services from the point of view of (a) the child (b) the parent/s or carer/s (c) the referring agency and (d) those providing the services; and

♦ to explore the relationship between Section 17 and Section 27 of the Children Act 1989.

Methods

The definitional and technical challenges involved in researching family support

The policy context

The choice of research methods was made against the background of the complexity of policy development in this area and in particular of the ideological framework of current legislation.

Most of the conceptual challenges of evaluating family support services arise from the value base and the specific requirements of the current legislative framework. The Children Act 1989 is underpinned by a set of principles, foremost of which are:

♦ the need to safeguard and promote the welfare of children within their own homes;

♦ the wide definition of 'child need';

♦ the positive value of involving many statutory, voluntary and community agencies across a range of professional disciplines;

♦ the importance of working in partnership with parents; and

♦ the supportive role of providing accommodation.

Definitions

Definition of family support

Deriving from this framework, the first task in the research was to define the term 'family support'. We chose to use the definition laid out by the Audit Commission (1994, p. 82): 'Any activity or facility provided either by statutory agencies or by community groups or individuals aimed to provide advice and support to parents to help them in bringing up their children.' This definition is also supported by Gibbons's work (1992) on family support.

Definitions may be parent/carer-centred or family-centred as well as child-centred: 'Family support is about the creation and enhancement, with and for families in need, of locally based (or accessible) activities, facilities and networks, the use of which have outcomes such as alleviated stress, increased self-esteem, promoted parental/carer/family competence and behaviour and increased parental/carer capacity to nurture and protect children.' (Hearn 1995, p. 6)

The services, whether provided singly or in packages of care, were classified as follows:

♦ social work support:
  • allocation to a social worker, offering short- or long-term, direct or indirect support
  • allocation to a family support worker, offering practical and emotional support on a day-by-day basis;

- child- and family-centred services: community care, accommodation, respite care, activities, day care; and

- other services: housing, Section 17 money, help with health and education services.

Definition of need

'Need' is a complex and socially constructed concept (Langdon 1998). 'The concept of need has always been too imprecise, too complex, too contentious to be a target for policy and therefore leaves a lot to be desired both as an epidemiological identifier and also as a basis for evaluating the performance of policies' (Bradshaw 1972, p. 640). Definitions of need – whether psychological or sociological – vary, as exemplified in Table 2.1.

Table 2.1 *Definitions of need*

Study	Definition of need
Maslow 1970	A hierarchy: physiological; safety; social; self-esteem; knowledge and understanding; self-actualisation
Bradshaw 1972	Expressed; felt; normative; comparative
Kellmer Pringle 1975	Love and security; new experiences; praise and recognition; responsibility
Ward 1995	Health; education; identity; family and social relationships; social presentation; emotional and behavioural development; self-care skills
Sinclair and Carr-Hill 1997	Intrinsic; parental illness; abuse/neglect; families under stress; offending behaviour; non-viable families; deprivation; other

The study incorporated the following categorisation of need, developed from the work of Sinclair and Carr-Hill (1997):

- intrinsic need – relating to children's own physical condition, developmental delay or difficulties; physical or mental illness; behavioural problems at home or at school;

- need because of parental illness – mental and physical; addiction; depression; or severe stress;

- need because of family stress, as a result of living within an unstable, conflictual, emotionally or developmentally damaging family;

- need because of offending behaviour – breaking the law; and

- need because of social deprivation – poverty or social disadvantage.

The same categories were used by Thoburn et al. (2000), because when the two studies were being undertaken these categories were being piloted by the Department of Health.

In Chapter 3 the content and meaning of these categories is described in detail, showing how they link to the characteristics of children in the study.

Challenges to data collection

The 1995 study on the Children Act had provided an overview of the national scene in England in respect of provision for children in need (Aldgate and Tunstill 1995). Its purpose was to present a broad picture of the range of approaches to implementing Section 17 of the Children Act 1989 that had been adopted by the majority of local authorities during the first 18 months of the Act's implementation.

The data collection process indicated that the local authorities' own data collection procedures were inadequate, disorganised and unsystematic. Quality of data collection was dependent on whether or not a team had collated figures and whether or not local audits had been carried out by internal or external agencies.

The data collected by the study were often so scattered, so varied in terms of sample size and so uncollated that they could not serve to provide a comprehensive picture of children in need in a local authority. When data were collected, it often remained uncollated and unanalysed. Problems arose both from a lack of computerisation and from the inadequate availability of research analysts.

Reports by the Social Services Inspectorate in December 1997 and 1999 were very critical of the failure of social services departments (SSDs) to meet the aims and objectives of Section 17, raising questions about the quality of monitoring undertaken and the information produced. Overall, management information was poor in most SSDs. Managers had little information about throughput of work or the demand being experienced at the front line.

Resource shortfalls were consistently not recorded so that the information was not available for future planning. Systems were insufficient to inform the wider picture of need in family support purposes.

> There was a consistent picture of poor work on measuring outcomes. This was associated with a lack of quality of monitoring and evaluation of complaints, or user surveys. . . . It would have helped the SSDs to identify the extent of demand for their services and what they had done well in order to develop effective family support services.

In designing the present study, account was taken of findings relating to the lack of availability of information. This underlined the importance of obtaining data directly from carers and children themselves as well as from social services personnel.

Another challenge is posed by the number of agencies which can and should play a role in providing family support. This challenge derives from the conviction that children's welfare needs are physical, intellectual, emotional, social and behavioural. Prior to the start of the current study, an audit of family support services in one local authority revealed a surprising (to the local authority) range of organisations and agencies involved. Local authorities may lack this type of knowledge, a deficiency that could be aggravated by a lack of shared perceptions between agencies and the lack of a common language in which to discuss *need*, *access* and *outcome*.

The clear encouragement in the legislation to develop a mixed economy of welfare, by maximising the partnerships between statutory, voluntary and private sectors, has conferred a potential commercial value on data that would not previously have been seen to carry significant financial implications. This *commercialisation* is likely to be an issue for statutory, voluntary and private organisations. It is also likely to complicate research tasks generally, in terms of negotiation of access; selection of appropriate research sites; presentation and dissemination of findings. As discussed above, in the case of this children in need study, some adjustments to the original design were made, but generally the implementation closely resembled the proposed design.

Interpretation of outcomes

As well as pressures from policy, there are technical problems associated with the assessment and interpretation of outcomes. All interventions are outcome-oriented. The political and professional justification of intervention into the privacy of the family has been the possibility that positive change will derive from such intervention. Traditionally, the success or failure of child-care social work has been measured in terms of a child ceasing to be abused, being reunited with the family or being found a new home.

It is essential to distinguish between output and outcome. Different approaches for doing this include:

- service-based and client-based (Cheetham et al. 1997);
- service and client levels of output (Hardiker et al. 1991); and
- intermediate and final outcomes (Knapp 1984) – indicators of performance, service or activity rather than indicators of effect, influence or impact; changes in individual well-being compared with levels of well-being in the absence of a caring intervention.

Outcomes may be viewed in various ways (Parker et al. 1991):

- public outcomes;
- service outcomes;
- professional outcomes;
- family outcomes; and
- outcomes for children.

The present study took account of the perspectives of parent/carers, children and social work professionals. A particular difficulty in evaluating outcomes for family support is that it cannot always be assumed that there are common interests in most families: keeping a family intact may be at the cost of the ill-treatment of a victimised member. Conversely, keeping a child at home may be at a cost to other members of the family.

However, in the context of Section 17, the study was concerned to identify outcomes in terms of services made available and the responses to those services by parents and children. Comparison of the problems, experience, backgrounds and attitudes of parents and children before and after intervention represented an indicator of change.

Data collection

The sample

The original purpose was to draw the sample of children and families from three local authorities concentrating on children in middle childhood. A pilot survey indicated two important findings:

- very few children in this age group were receiving family support services; and

- even more worryingly, family support services in the three local authorities we had intended to study were sparse.

In view of this we decided to extend the scope of the study to seven local authorities. These seven were chosen to incorporate a wide geographical and socio-economic spread, which would enable us to see whether the paucity of family support services was a local or, as we feared, a national problem. Although the result of depressing policy trends, these changes in design have strengthened the content of the study, because it meant that data were gathered across a wide and representative range of seven social services departments.

The seven local authorities who took part in the study comprised two metropolitan authorities, three London boroughs, and two county councils. There was a broad cross-section in terms of variables such as geographical location (North/Midlands/South), affluence, local governance by different political parties and size.

Ninety-three children were involved in the study. Table 2.2 shows the distribution across local authorities, some of which were chosen to maximise the likelihood of including respondents from a range of racial, ethnic and cultural backgrounds.

Table 2.2 *Distribution of the children across the local authorities*

Local authority	Number of children
London Borough 1	5
Metropolitan Authority 1	11
County 1	11
London Borough 2	11
London Borough 3	12
Metropolitan Authority 2	18
County 2	25

n=93

There were 23 children aged up to 6 years (12 boys and 11 girls) 47 children aged 7–12 years (34 boys and 13 girls) and 23 children aged 13–16 years (13 boys and 10 girls). Three cases were withdrawn from the data set during the course of the study as their circumstances changed and they were no longer eligible for inclusion.

How the children were selected for the study

Because children can be referred to Social Services for a range of reasons, a purposive sample of Section 17 cases was selected. This excluded the following:

♦ all children where the current primary referral was for the investigation of child maltreatment; and

♦ all children where the current primary referral was on the basis of a specific disability as defined in arm c) of Section 17.

Reasons for exempting these groups were as follows. Previous research (Little and Gibbons 1993; Thoburn et al. 1993; Sharland et al. 1996) pointed to large numbers of children being referred as 'child protection' cases but relatively small numbers being subsequently placed on Child Protection Registers or becoming the subject of Care Orders.

These groups were already the subject of extensive research (see, for example, Department of Health 1995) and accorded, if only initially, with the definitions of need in arms a) and b) of the Act. By comparison, there was a dearth of information about other children who were not referred in 'child protection terms' but who came to the attention of the police, had health- or school-related problems or were referred by those holding parental responsibility because they had behaviour problems.

These children could be seen as a 'marginal' group who were likely to test the system most. Little was known at the initial stage about their 'career' as children in need. In addition, the Aldgate and Tunstill 1995 Children Act study had also pointed to the fact that the least adequately understood implications of Section 17 related to service provision in respect of those children who might be reasonably expected to fall within the remit of arms a) and b) of the Children Act definition of children in need.

Both these arms were drafted into the Act to emphasise the value of earlier rather than later intervention. They were also intended to reflect the consensus that children's lives are multi-faceted and are vulnerable to the impact of many factors, including parental circumstances and problems, challenges to child and parental health and difficulties in school.

For clarification we reproduce the first two arms of Section 17:

a) he is unlikely to achieve or maintain, or to have the opportunity of achieving or maintaining, a reasonable standard of health or development without the provision for him of services by a local authority.

b)   his health or development is likely to be significantly impaired, or further impaired, without the provision for him of such services.

It was the wish of the researchers to cross the hitherto rigid boundaries between 'prevention' and 'protection' that had developed prior to the Children Act 1989. For this reason, from each social services department, over a specific period of six months, a purposive, sequential sample was taken of children referred to social services departments for services by professionals, families or the children themselves that fall under Part III of the Children Act 1989.

For this reason, further analysis and discussion in terms of ethnicity were impracticable. This lack of an ethnically representative sample was also identified as problematic in Gibbons's examination of family support services (1990).

Method of investigation

Parents or carers of 93 children took part in the study. A subset of 41 age-appropriate children were also interviewed:

♦   three children under 7;

♦   25 children aged 7–12; and

♦   13 children aged 13–16 years.

It was a central concern of the study to interview children, since the intention of the Children Act as a whole is that the children's own views should be heard; however, historically, less attention appears to have been paid to this expectation in respect of Section 17 than in the context of provision of, for example, accommodation or court procedures.

Eligible children were identified by social services staff at the point of referral. Referrals could be made by parents/carers, the children themselves, other family members and professional or non-professional agencies outside the family. Social services staff facilitated the participation of families by giving potential subjects a brief written explanation of the study, including what participation would be involved and details of how to enlist as a participant. This facilitation was essential for reasons of client confidentiality. Since details of families who declined to participate were unavailable, it was impossible to establish whether non-participating families differed significantly from those who took part.

Home interviews were carried out, the first interview aiming to elicit the background to the referral or request for services and the expectations of and attitudes to the services likely to be wanted or offered. Although it had originally been intended to interview both parents, the high proportion of single-parent families in the sample rendered this inappropriate. Instead of seeking additional views on the children's and families' problems and needs, more information was obtained in the form of qualitative data, thus enriching the quantitative data by placing it in the context of individual experience. Information on living circumstances and family members and family problems was also collected. All interviews were tape-recorded, with the permission of participants. Particular account was taken of the ethical considerations involved in gaining children's consent and dealing appropriately with information disclosed (Mahon et al. 1996). The same methods were adopted as used in Aldgate and Bradley (1999).

The main components of the parents'/main carers' interview schedules were:

- demographic data;

- family background, including relationships, residence, health and income details;

- aspects of the referral;

- access to Social Services;

- previous contact with Social Services;

- family problems and concerns;

- availability of informal support;

- child's problems; and

- expectations of and attitudes to Social Services.

Interviews with children were conducted in a way that was age-appropriate (James 1993; Alderson 1995; Morrow and Richards 1996). The main components of the children's interview schedules were:

- background – age, interests, etc.;

- worries about self and about family;

- contacts outside the home;

- family support network;

- expectations of and attitudes to Social Services;

- access to Social Services;

- information from Social Services; and

- involvement in and understanding of decision-making.

Approximately six months after the first interview with parents/carers and children, second interviews were carried out in the home to review the outcome of referrals, regardless of whether services were obtained.

The main components of the parent/main carers' second interview schedules were:

- details of (changes in) relationships, residence, family members, income, informal support, family health;

- family problems;

- family contact;

- children's problems;

- nature, duration and outcomes of the involvement of Social Services – provision and effect;

- nature, duration and outcomes of other agencies' involvement – provision and effect;

- stressors;

- review of expectations of and attitude to Social Services; and

- feelings of involvement.

The main components of the children's second interview schedules were:

- worries about self;

- contact outside the home;

- worries about the family;

- nature, duration and outcomes of the involvement of Social Services – provision and effect;

- nature, duration and outcomes of other agencies' involvement – provision and effect; and

- review of expectations of and attitude to Social Services.

To explore the perspective of Social Services, the relevant social workers were asked to complete a questionnaire, the main components of which were:

- source of referral;

- previous contact – reasons and outcomes;

- family problems;

- action taken;

- referral to other agencies;

- the role of Social Services; and

- decision-making.

Social workers' questionnaires were a major source of information on inter-agency collaboration.

Approaches to data analysis

The data were of two types:

- quantitative – the coded and directly numerical data from the interview schedules with parents and children; and

- qualitative – transcripts of the discussion elements of interviews with parents and children.

The numerical and coded data were processed using the Statistical Package for Social Sciences (SPSS) program. To measure the strength of associations, Chi-square was the main significance test and was used for coded, categorical data, such as frequencies of category of need groups/age and gender groups. T-tests and analysis of variance were used in between-group comparisons of numerical, ratio-scale data to investigate the interactions of variables. A significance level was set at 001.

Descriptive statistics such as means, modes and ranges were informative and provided a structure for more complex analyses, as well as basic information such as numbers of boys, girls, household members and income. Descriptive statistics were used to assess variables such as levels of formal and informal support, family membership and health problems, services wanted, and anticipated benefits of contact with Social Services.

Given that no significant differences were identified between the seven local authorities on any of the main variables in the study, data was aggregated on the following variables:

- the main categories of need;

- the children's problems;

- age and gender of the children;

- family problems;

- referral source;

- previous contact with Social Services;

- concerns over contact with Social Services;

- type, structure and duration of services requested/obtained;

- carers' state; and

- status of cases at the end of the study.

Case studies

Because of the small size of the sample and the large number of variables, quantitative analysis yielded few associations that were statistically significant. It was, therefore, decided that maximum transparency of data would be achieved through the use of illustrative case studies (Corrie and Zaklukiewicz 1985), which complemented the quantitative data but were also independent sources of information.

The case studies illustrated the nature of children's/families' problems, adding depth to the quantitative categorisation by representing their individuality. For example, the case studies served to emphasise the complexity of problems associated with family disruption and domestic violence.

Data such as descriptions of past events in the children's and carers' lives provided a context for current problems and needs. Similarly, data relating to the motivation of families to approach Social Services were derived particularly from the case studies, thus enabling exploration of themes such as motivation.

Based on transcripts of actual interviews, the qualitative analysis was data-driven. To some extent data-driven analysis could circumvent the problem of the researchers' preconceived ideas influencing the findings. Valuable contextualisation was provided by the real life experience and views of participants, both in relation to the study and in relation to the social services process. Similarly, investigation of data from three different but complementary sources (parent/carer, child, social worker) increased the scope of the investigation.

3 *The children in need and their families*

One consistently widespread finding of the last four decades has been the presence of multiple psycho-social problems in the backgrounds of children who enter the care system (Gray and Parr 1957; Packman 1968; Aldgate 1977; Bebbington and Miles 1989). For example, in their study of 2,500 children admitted to care, Bebbington and Miles found that, before admission, only a quarter were living with both parents; almost three-quarters of their families received income support; only one in five lived in owner-occupied housing; and over half were living in poor neighbourhoods.

Kumar (1993) links social class and reduced educational achievement by showing that children of working-class parents tend to make less progress within the primary school than other pupils. Thus, by the time of secondary school entry, gaps in achievement levels tend to widen, even among children of equal levels at primary school entry.

The research literature on health inequality inevitably links poverty, low income and inadequate housing conditions with the indicators on poor health and vulnerabilities to constant infection (Gibbons 1990; Bradshaw 1990; Kumar 1993). Additionally, Utting et al. (1993), having reviewed evaluation studies on a wide range of family support projects, conclude that there is an important link between family circumstances and the delinquent behaviour of children.

Notwithstanding the complexity of problems with more than one possible cause, the identification of predisposing factors remains a key issue. The debate concerning the possibility of predicting children at developmental risk is complex. The most potent factors have been identified as:

   ♦   inadequate supervision and inconsistent discipline;

   ♦   parental indifference and neglect;

   ♦   conflict between parents;

   ♦   parents who are/have been criminals; and

   ♦   low income (Utting et al. 1993).

Recent reviews continue to illuminate the widening gap between rich and poor in Britain since 1979 (Kumar 1993; Bradshaw et al. 1993). The largest increases in European child poverty have been shown to be in the United Kingdom and Ireland, a situation likely to have an impact on the population of 'children in need'.

This chapter describes the general characteristics of the children in the study and the families to which they belong.

Age and gender of the children in need

Twenty-three children in the study were aged up to 6 years; 47 were aged 7–12 years; 23 were aged 13–16 years. There were 59 boys in the study and 34 girls. Table 3.1 shows the distribution of children according to age and gender.

Table 3.1 *Age and gender of the study children*

Age group	Number	
	Male	**Female**
0–6	12	11
7–12	34	13
13–16	13	10
Total	**59**	**34**

n=93

Whilst the study children cannot be representative of all children in need in the UK, it is useful to set this gender ratio against other research findings which suggest that boys may show more expressive behaviour problems than girls. Boys have frequently been found to be ostensibly more troublesome than girls, manifesting overt aggressive behaviour problems and conduct disorders, whilst girls may retreat into depression and self-harm (Rutter 1970).

Boys, mostly in their middle years, were also likely to belong to families where there had been at least one previous contact with Social Services. In about half these cases, the previous contact had involved child protection concerns, ranging from low-key suspicions to statutory interventions, but very few cases had involved care proceedings.

Past events in the lives of the study children

A number of aspects of the children's past are contextually relevant:

- the births of some children had been difficult (4%), and in 14% of cases the parents had experienced difficulties with the child since birth in terms of behaviour;

- some children had been exposed to domestic violence in the past (11%); and

- some children had previous welfare histories, including a small subset of children in need who had a history of sexual abuse (9%) or had experienced other types of abuse (4%) and three children who had been in care in the past.

Difficult births and post-natal problems

Attachment issues between parents and children are relevant to a number of cases in the study where parents reported that birth-trauma and/or bonding problems that accompanied a mother's post-natal depression appeared to have impaired the parent–child relationship.

Underlying resentments appeared to have escalated into emotional abuse or rejection of the children. This, in turn, created a vicious circle of negative interaction that resulted in children's behavioural problems. Some children were on the borderline of risk of significant harm from over-stressed parents. One quotation serves to illustrate this type of situation. A mother said frankly of her 7-year-old son: 'I could never hold him like I could the other children when he was a baby.'

Domestic violence

Eleven per cent of the children had been exposed to domestic violence at some point, and the majority were under the age of 7 at the time of such exposure. They were more likely to have been referred to Social Services for reasons of poor mental health or serious problems than other children of a comparable age.

Previous welfare histories

A characteristic of over half of the children, particularly the boys, was that they were already known to Social Services or other similar agencies, although only three children had actually been received into care in the past.

Often, past agency contact had been for child protection reasons, resulting in either a low-key suspicion being investigated or in a higher-profile child abuse enquiry. It is probable that at least 14% of the children had actually suffered impairment or significant harm because of child abuse or neglect within the previous three years: substantiated child sexual abuse alone accounted for 9% of this subset.

Aside from safeguarding the children, by far the main reason for previous referrals had been the children's offending behaviour. Eleven per cent of the children in the study had been known through police referrals, and half of them had already encountered the juvenile justice system. These children were manifesting serious behavioural problems such as arson, burglary or serious criminal damage, as well as exhibiting behaviour problems within the home. Common pursuits included stealing from parents, shoplifting, vandalism and destruction of property.

Previous contact with Social Services had also resulted from ongoing problems of child behaviour associated with parenting problems. Children often emerged from disorganised families where parental mental health, violence, social deprivation, alcohol or drug misuse were well-known features.

At least half of the referrals in the study repeated earlier and similar requests for help with children that had not been alleviated on previous occasions. As children grew even more demanding, both physically and emotionally, the problems within families were likely to recur or exacerbate. New referrals were likely to be children in need through parental ill health.

Current problems for the study children

Apart from any problems their families might have, children themselves had a range of current problem areas, including physical and mental health needs, educational needs, disruptive behaviour, exclusion, disruption through home responsibilities, and peer relationship disruption.

The children's physical health needs

Chest conditions such as asthma or bronchitis were common among children in the study, often with the concomitant side effects of developmental problems such as deafness or speech impediment. A case study serves to illustrate an association between socio-economic factors and the development of a new-born baby:

● ●

A 10-week-old infant had an acute chest complaint compounded by the damp home environment in which she lived. The need was for re-housing support.

● ●

Examples of children with health needs include serious conditions such as kidney failure, developmental problems, epilepsy, asthma and chest complaints and other miscellaneous conditions, perhaps of psychosomatic origins, that impede development and maintenance of well-being. A comparative perspective of parents who were struggling with their own ill health added to the problems that threatened family life. It has been suggested that social isolation and lack of community child-care support may lead parents into both physical and depressive illness (Gibbons 1990).

The children's mental health needs

Many health problems were overlapping. There were serious problems, including eating disorders (obesity, anorexia or bulimia); substance abuse (alcohol, drugs, solvents); anxiety; phobic conditions; depression; low self-esteem; and psychotic illness such as acute schizophrenia.

Miscellaneous problems that characterised some of the children in the study were often indicators of anxiety or disturbance, such as:

♦ enuresis (7%); self-harming behaviour (2%); sleep disturbance (15%); and

♦ moodiness, temper tantrums or excessive aggression (16%).

A few children were at risk of harming themselves or endangering lives through their excessive destructive behaviour. For example, two children had committed arson, and one boy, who was eventually sent to a residential school, had nearly 'throttled' a child in the park with an iron bar. His father described how he was forced to intervene rapidly and how close he got to 'thrashing the living daylights' out of his son.

Educational disruption: behavioural

Behavioural problems were manifested in the school as well as in the home environment, affecting both performance and attendance.

Parents suggested that a third of the children were having behavioural problems within the school setting, with some actually lacking regular schooling as a result of truancy, exclusion or school refusal/phobia. Parentally condoned absences indicated neglect of parental responsibility and inadequate supervision or control of the children.

Similarly, school underachievement proved to be an issue where absence, poor concentration and lack of interest were common. In the context of a positive perception of schooling acting as a compensation for stresses within the home and as a protective factor in adverse social circumstances, both the nature and degree of educational disruption found in the study were significant among these children in need (Rutter 1985).

Children as young carers

There were four cases in which illness and/or hospitalisation of parents resulted in children taking on much of the responsibility for the household.

Intermittent school attendance was the price paid by the children who were the young carers of parents suffering from physical or mental disabilities. Case studies serve to illustrate the demands on young carers.

Two children aged 8 and 10 years carried out household tasks as a consequence of their mother's colostomy operation.

Two children were emotionally and physically supportive of a mother who was suffering from multiple sclerosis. In addition, these children had already experienced the trauma of divorce, a disastrous move abroad, fostering experiences and sexual abuse.

Problems with peers

A quarter of the children in the study seemed to be 'loners', revealing problems in social relationships within their peer groups or immediate social networks. Recent research has highlighted the beneficial outcome of the growing influence of the peer group on the healthy functioning of children (Levitt et al. 1993; Byng-Hall 1992). Successful socio-emotional relationships outside the immediate family may mitigate against adverse family circumstances. However, many children in need appeared unable to make or sustain friendships with their peers.

Bullying behaviour was evident, with children alternating between the roles of perpetrator and victim. Children were also vulnerable to racial harassment (6% of cases). In addition, two cases of serious school refusal were traced to underlying fears of bullying.

Poor social skills led some children into unsuitable peer relationships, including premature sexual relationships (5%), and there was one case of an under-age pregnancy.

The families of the children in need

Composition of the families

All the study children were living with at least one birth parent. Almost half the children lived in single-parent families, well over the national average of 25% and even higher than the 46% in a recent study of accommodated children (Packman and Hall 1998) or in other Children Act research examining family support provisions (Aldgate and Bradley 1999; Smith 1992).

Most commonly, there were two children per family (the average being 2.5 children per family). Lone children were the smallest group of children (19 cases). There were 42 families with three or more children, and the largest family had eight children.

Many children had experienced the break-up of their parents' relationship and the reconstitution of families:

- ◆ less than half of the parents were in a relationship (44%);

- ◆ half of the parents were not in a relationship at the time of the study; and

- ◆ 6% of the parents were in 'on/off' relationships, i.e. the other parent (generally the father) was present and often staying in the home, but the status was unclear – an ambiguity possibly related to eligibility for benefits.

Forty-four per cent of the parents were in a relationship: 30% were married (20% were parents to all the children in the family and 10% were in a second or further relationship); 4%, previously married, were living with a new partner; 10% had never married (3% had had one relationship and 7% more than one relationship). Fifty per cent of the parents were not in a relationship at the time of the study: 38% were divorced or separated and living alone; 12% had never married and were living alone.

Marital breakdown or other family disruption

Almost half of the children had experienced a change of parents in reconstituted families in the three years prior to the study, either losing a parent (usually the father) through marital separation and/or gaining a stepparent as a result of a new marital (or similar) partnership.

Changing parental relationships led to a tenth of the children experiencing difficulties with the new parental figure. Just under half of these cases were reported to be seriously problematic. Contact issues with the absent parent were often problematic, too: more than a quarter (27%) of parents interviewed highlighted this as a major problem.

Within this scenario of disharmonious marital relationships, children were subject to emotional stress or abuse, sometimes acting as scapegoats for the warring parents. Allegations between parents of child abuse or neglect were not uncommon. In a few cases, children were effectively passed between warring parents; in one case there was a kidnapping.

There were between one and three adults per household, most frequently one (53 cases). In two-thirds of the cases where second adults were present, both adults were parents of all the children in the household; in just over one-quarter of the cases, they were stepparent to at least some of the children in the household. The rest were unrelated to the children.

Relationship problems

Although less than half of the families of children in need were headed by a couple, nearly two-fifths of all the families in the study were having severe relationship problems, including with absent partners. Just over one-tenth of the children had experienced domestic violence.

A third of the children had recently moved house: either changed which parent they lived with or, more commonly, the parental home had changed.

The study parents

The parents who participated in the study were generally female (88%) and the majority were aged from mid-20s to mid-30s (see Table 3.2). From the data available, the average age of parents' partners was also estimated to be 32 years (table not shown).

Table 3.2 *Age of the parents*

Age range	Number
< 20	3
20–25	10
26–30	28
31–35	24
36–40	15
41–45	7
45–62	6

n=93

Past events in the parents' lives

A number of aspects of the parents' past are contextually relevant:

♦ a subset of parents had experienced abuse in the past – sexual abuse (4%), other abuse (8%);

♦ a subset of parents had experienced domestic violence (10%);

♦ a small subset of parents had been in care as a child (3%); and

♦ a tenth of the parents came from homes where their parents had separated, causing them significant childhood problems.

The parents' own experience of childhood abuse and residential care could have affected their own parenting abilities. Qualitative data from the study indicate that parents who had themselves been in care felt that their experience made them determined to be good parents. Requesting support from Social Services was for them a positive step in the parenting process in order to avoid family failure and breakdown.

Criminal activity

A small subset of parents had a recent criminal history and/or problems with substance abuse. Qualitative analysis of interview data shows that relatively few parents were 'career criminals'. Encounters with the law had usually been over petty matters within the juvenile justice system. However, the few exceptions included offences relating to drugs and assaults. One single father from a very deprived background had 'seen every tough prison in the country', having been involved in armed robberies and other heavy offences in the past.

Ethnicity of the families of children in need

In multi-racial Britain, ethnic minority children and families may have needs associated with social exclusion (Amin and Oppenheim 1992; Barn et al. 1997). Indeed, ethnic minority school children have been subject to bullying and racial attacks.

It is also known that the emerging influence of the extended family, peers or the community on children in the middle years becomes more significant and influential within other cultural experiences (Byng-Hall 1992). The low take-up of services by minority groups has been of concern for some time. Minority families may be inhibited from asking for help outside their own community or family circle. Recent research into the provision of short-term accommodation found that only 8% of the children in the study were from ethnic minority families and located one of the difficulties as lack of appropriate publicity (Aldgate and Bradley 1999).

Other studies have suggested problems of comprehension and language, allied with the fear of formal processes and organisations having a negative impact on family life. In addition, a sense of pride may have impeded requests for appropriate help (Cleaver and Freeman 1995; Freeman and Hunt 1998).

In this study variations in the patterns of ethnicity were measured by establishing the parental racial origin. Table 3.3. show that the majority of the families in the study were white British, i.e., the study did not access a significant number of referrals from ethnic minority groups.

Table 3.3 *Ethnic origins of the families in the study*

Ethnic origin	Number
African	2
Pakistani	2
White British	81
Other European	3
Black British	3
Mixed	2

n=93

Ethnic minority families comprised 13% of the study sample, a figure that compares favourably with other studies on family support (see, for example, Thoburn et al. 2000) and was representative of the mean of percentages of ethnic minority families across the seven study areas. The scope of this study did not permit detailed investigation of any particular need of ethnic minority families, but the qualitative data suggested that their needs in relation to services for their children were similar to those of other families. For example, many families were concerned about their children's behaviour. More detailed work on family support and the needs of ethnic minority families receiving family support services is provided by Thoburn et al. 2000.

Extended families and support networks

Extended families

There has recently been discussion of the links between family breakdown and adverse family circumstances in which stresses or supports in the local environment are likely to influence parental functioning (Bebbington and Miles 1989; Cleaver et al. 1999; Gibbons 1992). This study of children in need reinforced these findings with evidence of the specific problems facing lone parents, such as social isolation, depression and financial hardship.

Just over two-fifths of the families in the study had at least a minimal local support network, but there was still a gap between what the informal network provided and what families actually needed. More than three-quarters of the families had at least one relative living less than five miles away. The nearest relative of one-tenth of the families lived more than 20 miles away; the nearest relatives of a few families (9%) lived between five and ten miles away; and 3% of the nearest relatives lived ten to twenty miles away.

Support networks

Table 3.4 indicates the sources of support available to the families. As can be seen, the quality of support varied: family was the main source of support; friends and GPs were a widespread resource; neighbours were a less likely source of help.

Table 3.4 *Sources of support available to the families*

Source of support	% of cases
Friends	48
Family	60
Neighbours	26
GP	44
Health visitor	34
Family centre	3

n=93

Homes of the children in need

Half of the families of children in need had housing problems, the majority of which were severe. Problems were due to unsatisfactory accommodation and unsatisfactory location.

Two-thirds of the children lived in rented local authority accommodation; the rest were more or less evenly spread across privately rented accommodation, housing associations and owner-occupancy. Two-thirds lived in houses, the rest in flats or other types of accommodation.

A third of the children had moved house, often at no great distance from their original dwellings, but this nevertheless involved the children in forging links in the new neighbourhood and in changing schools.

Although relatively geographically stable, nevertheless the children who moved could have experienced disruption and unhappiness as loss, particularly when also confronted with their parents' marital breakdown. In some cases marital breakdown involved the child in going to live with the formerly excluded parent. The findings suggest that almost half of the parents in the study thought that experiences of loss from bereavement and separation within the previous five years had been the catalyst for the children's emotional or behavioural problems and their own inability to cope. A case study serves to illustrate:

● ●

A 12-year-old boy was, according to his parents, unmanageable, and they wanted him to be accommodated. They felt that the root of his problems lay in poor bonding experiences with his mother. However, his behaviour had further deteriorated on the death of his grandfather, who had spent a great deal of leisure time with the boy.

● ●

Incomes of the study families

More than half of the families of children in need were experiencing severe financial problems (62%); less than a quarter were without financial problems (22%). Unemployment was common.

Eighty-two per cent of the main parents of the children did not work; 11 worked part-time. There was a pattern of long-term unemployment (70%), relative poverty and deprivation, exacerbated by growing children straining families' limited resources. In turn, children were affected by family stresses arising from poverty. Only two-fifths of the single parents were receiving maintenance payments for their children from absent fathers via the Child Support Agency.

Average weekly income was £152.21, which was below the level of income recommended by the Child Poverty Action Group at the time the data was gathered (Middleton, Ashworth and Walker 1994). In almost two-thirds of the homes there was no wage earner, and the average income was £122.81 per week. In 15% of the homes, there was one full-time worker (average weekly income £153.18). In one-tenth of the homes, there was one part-time work-er (average weekly income £165.02).

Whereas the majority of families received income support, a minority of families had somewhat higher incomes: eight families (9%) earned in excess of £200 per week. Generally these families had two wage earners, one part-time, the other full-time. The principle breadwinner would generally be employed in unskilled or semi-skilled work in such industries as car manufacture, printing and construction.

Health of the study families

Table 3.5 shows that around half of the families in the study had a family member with some sort of chronic health problem, with a subset receiving long-term or recurrent hospital in-patient treatment. In addition to the serious health problems presented in Table 3.5, half of the families also had regular minor health problems (particularly asthma); and minor mental health problems (for example, mild depression).

The findings indicate a high level of parents whose ability to cope was impaired by depression. It could be that the children's unmanageable behaviour, one of the major problems in the study, was less a reason for the intervention of Social Services' than parental distress or depression. However, in either situation, the children were in need of such intervention.

Parents also suffered from health problems likely to reduce their coping abilities, such as:

♦ eating disorders;

♦ gynaecological disorders;

♦ migraine; and

♦ back ache.

Table 3.5 *The families' health problems*

Health problem	% of cases
Chronic mental	12
Chronic physical	43
Chronic mental and physical	3
Hospitalisation: physical, short-term	23
Hospitalisation: mental, short-term	1
Hospitalisation: physical, long-term	16
Hospitalisation: mental, long-term	3
Parent(s) with learning disabilities	2
Restricted mobility of parent(s)	23
Child(ren) with learning disabilities	12
Child(ren) with asthma	14

n=93

Summary: the children

Half of the children in the study were aged 7–12 years and were likely to have behavioural and emotional problems; a quarter of the children were under 7 years of age and likely to be in need due to family stress and the mothers' ill health; a quarter of the children were aged 13–16 years and likely to have behavioural/control problems, including substance abuse and offending.

There were more boys (59) than girls (34). Boys were more likely to have had a history of welfare.

Summary: the families

Almost half of the families were headed by single parents; half had experienced recent changes to the family structure; and there were relationship problems in over one-third. A third of the children had recently moved. Over two-fifths of the parents connected an experience of loss through bereavement/separation to their children's behavioural and emotional problems.

The main parents of children were mostly female (88%), aged from mid-20s to mid-30s (81%) and white British (87%). Incomes were low – on average, £152.21 per week; 70% were long-term unemployed; 50% had health problems in the family.

Family, friends and doctors were their main sources of support.

4   The children's problems and categories of need

Definitions within the Children Act 1989 relating to family support

Given that the objective of this study is to explore the provision of services within Part III of the Act, it is helpful to recap and expand on relevant definitions. Section 17 of the Children Act 1989 states that a child is 'in need' if:

(a)   he is unlikely to achieve or maintain, or to have the opportunity of achieving or maintaining, a reasonable standard of health or development without the provision for him of services by a local authority;

(b)   his health or development is likely to be significantly impaired, or further impaired, without the provision for him of such services; or

(c)   he is disabled [Category of need outside the scope of the study].

Additionally, the *Guidance and Regulations* states:

The definition of need . . . is deliberately wide to reinforce the emphasis on preventive support to families. It has three categories: a reasonable standard of health or development; significant impairment of health or development and disablement. It would not be acceptable for an authority to exclude any of these three – for example, by confining services to children at risk of significant harm which attracts the duty to investigate under Section 47. (DoH 1991, para. 2.4)

Classification by need of the cases in the study

The five categories of need outlined in Chapter 2 were developed from the work of Sinclair and Carr-Hill (1997) and were used to classify the cases in the study. We did this by selecting the key reason for referral to Social Services given by the respective referrers.

Intrinsic need

This category encompassed the needs of all the families that included a child who had some intrinsic impairment, an impairment that would almost certainly have been present whatever the context but might be coped with better by some families than by others. The determinant of demand on Social Services was manifest parental need for support, although the underlying need would be the child's intrinsic condition. Sub-categories were likely to include the various diagnostic categories ascribed to the children through medical and/or educational assessment.

Parental ill health

This category covered situations where a child was in need because the carer was unable to be effective as a result of a condition intrinsic to themselves – being too disabled or ill, either permanently or temporarily, to adequately meet the child's needs through the discharge of their parental responsibilities.

This category would exclude chronic social incapacity or inadequacy that could not be attributable to a diagnosable medical condition. It would include young carers taking premature responsibility for caring for a parent or adult family member. It would also include the needs of children arising out of living with an alcoholic or mentally ill parent.

Families under stress

This category encompassed need arising not only from a 'bad patch' experienced by families who normally functioned adequately, but also from parenting deemed by referrers to be chronically unsatisfactory. Potentially regarded as a stigmatising category, none the less it represented the reality of life for children who were suffering developmentally because of the emotional and relational context of their family life.

It included inter-parental conflict, tensions consequential to separation or divorce; and 'pathological' family dynamics. It is probable that, if unmet, need manifested within this category could develop into other forms of need such as offending behaviour or abuse/neglect.

Offending behaviour

Although offending behaviour may well be associated with other categories of need, it was clear that it represented a discrete set of reasons for the involvement of Social Services.

Social deprivation

Social deprivation was present in other categories of need, particularly in the case of needs that were intrinsic to carers and children and needs arising from family stress. For example, young single parents had difficulty coping because their income was low rather than because they were young. In this study, it was treated as a discrete category of need, based on the carers' own reports of the most significant aspect of the situation that brought them into contact with Social Services.

Figure 4.1 illustrates the distribution of families with children in need across the five categories of need. It is clear that the largest group of children in the study were in need because of family stress; the second largest because of social deprivation. Children in need because of offending behaviour were the smallest group, probably because of the availability of other systems to deal with delinquency.

Figure 4.1 *Number of families by category of need*

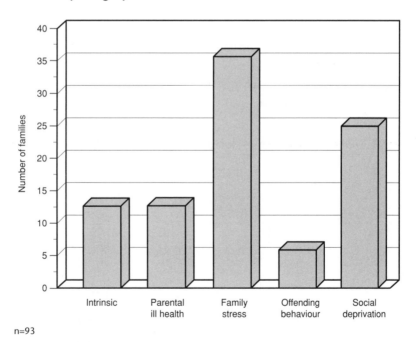

n=93

Table 4.1 shows that there were more boys than girls in the study as a whole and across all categories of need except social deprivation. This gender ratio can be set against other research findings and suggests that boys may externalise their problems and react more quickly to family stress than girls (Rutter

1970). Therefore, it is perhaps not surprising that, in this study, it was the behaviour of boys that more often led families to Social Services.

Figure 4.2 shows the relationship between the categories of need and childrens' ages.

Table 4.1 *Categories of need according to the children's gender*

	Intrinsic	Parental ill health	Family stress	Offending behaviour	Social deprivation	Total
Male	9	8	25	6	11	59
Female	4	5	11	–	14	34

n=93

Younger children (up to 6 years)

Figure 4.2 shows that more than a third of the families of the youngest children had approached or been referred to Social Services because of a range of family stresses. Sometimes these had escalated into crises that challenged the families' abilities to cope. Family stress, in the form of conflictual or new relationships created strains on the family system, leaving parents feeling 'at the end of their tether' and reducing the quality of their parenting.

Figure 4.2 *Number of children by category of need, according to age groups*

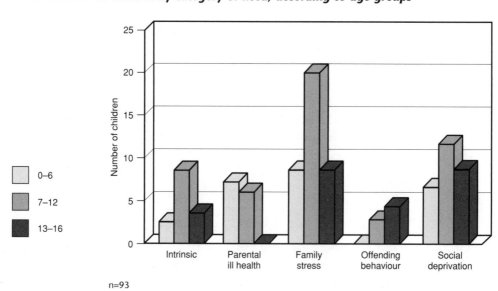

n=93

Almost a third of the cases in the youngest age group involved need due to parental ill health, often occurring as mental health problems such as eating disorders or drug abuse. The strains of poverty and social deprivation were apparent in about a quarter of the families of the youngest children.

A case study serves to illustrate the complexity of need:

● ●

A refugee mother of three children under 5 years of age was a victim of serious domestic violence. She left her partner to escape initially to a women's refuge, although later she was re-housed in poor surroundings, far away from her former social network. She not only felt socially isolated, but was also suffering from depression, paranoia and low self-esteem. Her previous standard of living had been reduced to social security benefits or handouts from the local mosque. She found the children's distressed behaviour difficult to cope with and elicited help and advice from Social Services, who responded by putting in a fully supportive care package to prevent the possibility of accommodation.

● ●

Children in their middle years (7–12-year-olds)

Figure 4.2 shows that the most common needs of children in this age group, almost three-quarters of whom were boys, arose from family stress. In this age group were more than half of the cases of intrinsic need, a category that covers a range of developmental childhood difficulties such as behavioural problems, medical conditions or educational delays.

Offending behaviour was restricted to boys in their middle and older years. Need through parental ill health concerned children in their early and middle years, possibly because it was sometimes taken for granted that they would act as a carer for the sick parents or could look after themselves.

Instances of problems related by parents involved issues of management and control within the home and school, or behaviour such as bullying, tantrums, bed-wetting, self-harming and running away. Some of this behaviour was explained by the parents as a response to stress, for example the reaction to a parent leaving the family home. Other behaviour was less easy for parents to understand and may have related to children's health or developmental problems, which the parents felt unable to manage any longer on their own.

Although many of these families had chronic problems as a whole, and the child's behavioural problems were likely to be related to family distress, the nature of the referral frequently indicated that parents were struggling to manage their children. Inevitably, such difficulties were likely to upset family dynamics and interfere with the well-being of other siblings. Almost a third of the parents claimed that sibling relationships were difficult to manage alongside the tantrums or behaviour of the child designated as 'in need'.

Entering adolescence (12–16 years)

As can be seen from Figure 4.2, offending behaviour was predominant in the group of older children, and accounted for two-thirds of the children in this category. Other parental concerns centred on the state of their children's mental health problems, again often manifested as behavioural or control difficulties (for example, due to substance abuse or rebelliousness). These problems were often linked with the children's poor educational performance, truancy or school exclusion, and inevitably contributed to family stress. A case study serves to illustrate the serious nature of the children's problems:

• •

The 13-year-old son of a reasonably affluent couple who were in the throes of separating started behaving in a bizarre fashion after excessive drug-taking. The problem first came to their notice when the police found him sleeping rough. For two years he had been unmanageable, misusing drugs, shoplifting and showing acute signs of psychosis. By the time he was 15 he was in an adult psychiatric unit. Social Services were intending to find a more suitable placement for him.

• •

Having briefly explored the relationship between the categories of need and the children's gender and age, we now describe what the categories of need represented in terms of the circumstances and problems that had led families to the door of Social Services.

Intrinsic need

There were 13 children with intrinsic needs of three main types:

> ♦ multiple problems encompassing health, education and social needs – seven children, all boys, aged over 7 years;

- educational problems, generally associated with behavioural problems at home – four children (three boys and one girl), all aged over 7 years; and

- physical health problems – two children (one boy and one girl), both under 5.

Multiple problems

In the cases of the seven children with problems associated with multiple intrinsic needs, the parents were often desperate to obtain help from any professional source: education services, health or social services. The behavioural problems of the children were often extreme, including tantrums; destructive, violent and intimidating behaviour, particularly towards siblings; drug or alcohol abuse.

All the children with intrinsic needs were experiencing problems with schooling. Three of the children were out of mainstream education at the time of referral, having been excluded because of their behaviour. For example, a 15-year-old boy had been expelled for setting fire to a girl's hair. The other four children were in danger of exclusion for a number of reasons, including behavioural problems and learning difficulties. Some had difficulties such as dyslexia and dysgraphia, which, accompanied by an inability to concentrate, made their progress at school very difficult.

Educational problems

Four children were experiencing educational problems as the main cause of need (although, as described above, educational problems also permeated other categories):

- school refusal because of fears of bullying;

- lack of ability to learn;

- general 'school phobia'; and

- behavioural problems.

In three of the four cases, although education welfare services were involved, parents wanted supplementary support from Social Services for the behavioural problems of the children. Case studies will serve to illustrate the children's educational problems:

A 9-year-old twin had learning difficulties which meant that her mother had reluctantly agreed to allow her to go to a special school. The school was not local and the girl lost touch with her friends, unlike her twin sister who remained at the local school. The child had difficulty mixing with other children as her social age did not match her mental age, and she intimidated the younger children with whom she was on the same mental wavelength. She reacted extremely badly to the change, becoming violent and aggressive in the home, although the school had no problems with her. Her mother commented: 'When she comes home I have to brace myself . . . it can be really, really awful.'

● ● ●

A 9-year-old girl had a history of school non-attendance: she had recently spent 18 months out of school. She had hearing problems that affected her schooling when she was younger, and as a result of this she had been teased. She now had a fear of going to school, which manifested itself in eating problems and diarrhoea. She was often late for school or when taken to school would not stay. Her teacher was not sympathetic. The child had contact, but not a good relationship, with the education welfare service.

Children's physical health problems

Two children had physical health problems and needs. One was a 10-week-old infant suffering from acute chest complaints that were compounded by damp home conditions. As well as wanting some help with housing to deal with the problem of her child's health, the mother wanted some kind of general support.

The other child had epilepsy, which was the trigger for referral to Social Services. However, the family as a whole was experiencing problems such as housing, poor parental health, marital discord and low parental self-esteem, for which general support was wanted.

Parental ill health

In all 13 cases in the study, it was the ill health of the mother that affected the children in a number of ways, including:

♦ the inability of the mothers to carry out household tasks;

- the inability of the mothers to care for their children; and

- the necessity for the children to act as young carers.

All the children in the study who were categorised as in need because of parental ill health were aged under 12 years; eight of them were boys. Problems could be:

- chronic physical health;

- acute physical health; and

- mental health.

Chronic physical health problems

Four mothers had chronic physical health problems such as multiple sclerosis, diseased colon and physical disability. Their health problems effectively precipitated their children into the role of young carers. Three mothers were single parents who had varying levels of informal support, with the result that their children experienced a range of negative effects:

- They had to carry out household tasks.

- Their ability to go out, particularly as a family, was seriously restricted or non-existent.

- They had to see their mother suffer.

The following case studies illustrate the problems arising from chronic physical ill health:

● ●

The long-term care of two children aged 9 and 11 was the focus of concern of a mother who had multiple sclerosis and was likely to die in the near future. She commented:

I can cope with the fatigue and as I said it's something that's part of everyday living now. You tend to get used to it. You tend to worry sometimes when you have little niggles. You wonder if it's the result of a relapse. I've had quite a few admissions to hospital . . . The problem is if I have a relapse and have to go into hospital the uncertainty it would cause for the duration of the stay. Sometimes it can be a few days, sometimes weeks; it could be even longer. Fortunately, there have been friends that have had the children, but one in particular kept coming and asking me when I was going home. You get stressed out thinking: 'Should I go home?' And you get uptight because you think: 'I don't want to cause her any problems', and that doesn't help your recovery if you've had a relapse and you're just more tense and more upset.

Her children had to carry out more household tasks than she would have liked them to have to do, and they also had to witness her being ill in circumstances which, given the choice, she would rather have avoided.

● ● ●

Two children aged 8 and 10 were affected by their mother being virtually housebound as a result of Crohn's disease and an unsuccessful colostomy. Her husband had been unable to cope with her illness and had left.

She felt that the children suffered because of her illness. She was also concerned because they had moved from a sheltered rural area to one where the children were more street-wise, and she felt that she could not give her own children the freedom that other children enjoyed. The children were seldom able to go out with her:

Everything is, 'Wait and see how mum is' and the situation can change from one hour to the next, so we could say, 'Right, we'll go to the pictures', and then five minutes before we're due to go out of the door: 'We can't go because Mum's got a problem.' And there's times when we've actually got where we're going to go and have had to go home because I'm not well.

The mother was also concerned that the children saw her being ill:

There are days when I can't keep any food down, so they'll see me being sick, they'll see a flare-up when my colostomy won't work properly, and they see a lot that, out of choice, I wish they didn't have to see.

She was also concerned that her illness put her children under stress:

I think they have the worry of me. It would be nice if they didn't have that worry of 'Mum's not well today', or 'Mum's got to go back into hospital'. They've put up with a lot. If I were still married it would be different . . .
I heard one of them say to my mum the other day: 'It's horrible seeing Mummy cry when she's not very well.' In a lot of ways I keep a lot back because I don't want to upset them or hurt them.

● ●

Acute physical health problems

Four mothers had acute physical health problems, including personal injury, a gall bladder complaint and birth complications. All had young children aged 2 or 3 years. Mostly, their ability to care practically for these children was impaired by:

♦   lack of mobility/use of limbs; and

♦   hospitalisation.

Case studies illustrate the impact of acute parental health problems on children:

● ●

A 12-year-old child was more or less unmanageable, and the situation was aggravated when his mother broke her wrist in a car accident.

● ● ●

A 3-year-old child was cared for by his young single mother whose family was in Africa, where she herself could not return for custody reasons and because of threats made by her husband. She had an appointment for an operation to remove a gallstone and was worried:

I hadn't got anyone who could look after my daughter, so I had to go to Social Services, to find foster care to look after her. My mother came over months ago because of my operation. I didn't know when but the doctor said 'soon'. My mother came over and stayed for a couple of months, but then my father had a heart attack, so she had to go back. I was so worried because if I died I had no family to look after my child.

● ●

Mental health problems

Five mothers of young children had mental health problems; in three cases the problem was post-natal depression of some sort:

♦   recurring bouts of depression;

♦   physical health needs in conjunction with post-natal depression; and

♦   attachment problems in conjunction with post-natal depression.

Since the children were very young, the negative effects of their situation were not particularly evident, but long-term effects were a source of concern. In addition, the mothers' problems diminished their ability to care for their new babies. A case study serves to illustrate the impact of parental mental health problems on children:

• •

A newly born baby was cared for by young parents, of whom one was disabled through back problems and the other had learning difficulties. The mother suffered physical health problems during the birth and then post-natal depression, to such an extent that the hospital felt that she urgently needed help to look after the baby. The mother was constantly exhausted and irritable, and the situation was taking its toll on the marital relationship.

• •

Families under stress

The most significant reason for approaching Social Services, family stress negatively affected 36 children in the study and represented the largest category of need. Problems of family stress could be long-term, short-term and situation-specific.

Children in need because of family stress were of five main types:

- children with young mothers at crisis point;

- children within families in conflict because of disagreement between their parents;

- children within families in conflict caused by the break-up and/or reconstitution of the family;

- children with behavioural problems; and

- children in families with multiple problems.

Young mothers at crisis point

Six mothers had come to Social Services at crisis point, unable to cope with the care of their children. They had all recently suffered a breakdown in their marital relationship or partnership, were suffering from depression and had young children under the age of 5 years. Their situations were aggravated in various ways:

- three of the mothers were coping with new babies;

- three of the mothers had been involved with soft or hard drugs;

- one of the mothers suffered from bulimia; and

- some of the mothers had other problems specific to the children in need, for example asthma, cleft palate, dislocated hip, being 'accident prone'.

Their children were reported to be unmanageable and the mothers felt over-whelmed by their situations: 'I just wanted to disappear. That's why the health visitor called the Social Services in, because I wasn't even bothered about him. I just wanted to go.'

Children were often described as 'sensing' the atmosphere and 'playing up on it'. This behaviour was, in some cases, noted in older siblings too. As a mother commented on a child who had daily tantrums and tried to run away: 'She knew I was depressed and would wind me up. I couldn't look after myself, never mind the children.' A case study illustrates the situation of young mothers at crisis point:

· ·

The mother of a 3-year-old child had a good support network from her family. However, she had been involved in a difficult relationship with a man and used soft drugs. The relationship having ended, and feeling very depressed, she found her daughter difficult to handle. She felt that her daughter was 'playing her up', and she couldn't get the attention she needed: 'I was smacking her and I had a fear of it getting out of control.'

· ·

Families in conflict

Children in nine families were considered to be in need because they were:

- experiencing conflict or disagreement between parents; and

- reacting to the reconstitution or the demise of their family.

Conflict between parents

Five children were, to varying degrees, the focus of their parents' concern because of the adverse effects of the behaviour of ex-partners. For example, in some families, there were disputes between parents over who should care for the children. A case study serves to illustrate a moderate situation, one whereby approaching Social Services was precautionary rather than desperate:

• •

A 10-year-old boy was being passed from one partner to the other. The mother had obtained a court order for custody of the child, and then decided that she could not look after him. The father turned to Social Services to ensure that the mother could not just turn up and take the child back again, as the situation was upsetting the child.

• •

Other cases were more alarming: contact with the ex-partner having led to visible disruption and distress within the children's lives. A case study serves to illustrate more severe problems through disagreements over care arrangements:

• •

An 8-year-old boy was not returned to his mother after a routine visit to his father. The father bribed the son with presents and denied the mother access to him, although she had always been responsible for his care. She resorted to snatching him back. The child was very distressed, throwing tantrums and scratching his face.

• •

Changes in the family structure

Four children had behavioural problems relating to their family situation, although the relationship between parents was not primarily a problem. In stepfamilies, particularly those constituted after a history of domestic violence, the children could be defiant and disobedient, with difficulties relating to their parents and/or stepparents. Problems could arise at school or at home: a boy who had previously been exposed to domestic violence started assaulting his mother; others were disruptive at school. Case studies serve to illustrate the impact on children of changes within the family:

• •

A 10-year-old boy, one of four children, had recently experienced change in the family structure when his mother remarried and the family moved to another area, although even before moving he had begun to react badly to the situation: he set fire to the next-door neighbour's garden. The behavioural problems had arisen recently, but his mother said:

He has always been a loner. He has problems making friends, he's not a mingler, he would rather be on his own . . . He won't go to sleep. Every time it's bedtime that's it, he starts . . . he's in a bad mood all the time. He has tantrums, he smashes the place up, he smashes his bedroom up. He's really violent, to say he's only 10. He's a big lad. He hits his stepdad now, and knows his stepdad won't hit him back. He punches him in the face. He kicks me. He does everything he possibly can . . . it involves everybody, I mean, he hates me, he's always telling me to die. He's just in a continual bad mood all the time.

I've got three others to cope with. It's disrupting their lives as well. Because they see him getting away with things they wouldn't be able to get away with, because I can't discipline him, because he won't do what I tell him . . . He bullies his younger sister and brother. He doesn't like his sister at all. She's a year younger but she's a lot smaller. He's always hitting her. She follows me about the house like a lost sheep . . . Last week he actually split her eye open, so he's getting a bit too much, really.

At school he had problems too:
He refuses to do a lot of schoolwork but at the moment he is being statemented. He has difficulties with his reading and writing.

● ● ●

A 15-year-old boy, had a difficult relationship with his stepfather, whose style was authoritarian. There were frequent arguments, and the stepfather felt that the boy could do better at school. The stepfather commented:
A stepfamily has its problems. I've always tried to be as fair as possible, but I'm sure my wife will sometimes say that I'm not . . . Whenever we have a row, it's not a major incident. We spark each other off. He's no worse I'm sure than any other teenage boy . . . We argued. He stormed out and ended up at the Social Services wanting to see someone, very upset. The first thing we knew about it was when we had a 'phone call. It all came out that he was upset about the way he had been rejected by his own father.

● ●

Children with behavioural problems

Nine children manifested problems that their parents found hard to manage. There were a number of ways in which this could occur. Parents were:

♦ generally unable to relate to and discipline their children;

- ♦ unable to deal with very specific problems with the behaviour of their children; and

- ♦ erratic in the way they related to and disciplined their children.

The behavioural problems exhibited by these children varied considerably. The two youngest children, a boy and a girl, were defiant and would not listen to their parents, who were inconsistent in their parenting. Other children were displaying extreme behavioural problems and were uncontrollable, being violent at home and at school and misusing alcohol and drugs.

The parents' hasty and negative reactions to the children's behaviour often compounded the problems they were trying to resolve. For example, a mother who shouted at her young children at the slightest provocation set up a pattern in her children of not listening and misbehaving. Case studies serve to illustrate the impact of inappropriate and inadequate parenting styles on children:

● ●

A 7-year-old boy was very disruptive at school and his parents could not manage him at home. He was involved with older children and had stolen money from a neighbour and a lighter from his mother, which he used for lighting fires in fields near his home.

● ● ●

Two children of middle years were controlled only with great difficulty by their mother. The family had a good support network, but the mother, having just gone through a particularly painful divorce, was suffering from lack of confidence in her ability to manage the children on her own. This was in spite of the fact the children were both bright and had no problems at school. However, the 10-year-old boy had been involved with the police on one occasion when 'he got in with the wrong crowd' and occasionally played truant; the 11-year-old daughter was rude and defiant. The mother had contacted Social Services about her son:

He was getting into a lot of trouble years ago because of where we were living . . . The social worker did actually contact me a bit too late, but it's a good job he did really because it's my daughter who needs one really. She's just naughty. She's got a mouth on her. She won't do as she's told. We don't get on at all. I've tried to get on. She cut her hair last night for nothing. She sat there in a tantrum, chopping away. It's a good job she's got thick hair.

The children fight and are very spiteful [even though] they are brother and sister. I think she has these mood swings . . . and it's worse for me really, you know, trying to split them up from fighting . . . My daughter is just very stubborn. I can't talk to her and neither can my mum or my sister. She's 11 going on 18. She says to me: 'You can't tell me what to do. I'm not a kid any more.' Sometimes I feel like smacking her; but to be honest, if I did start smacking her, I wouldn't stop, that's how mouthy she is; but it doesn't solve your problems anyway does it? She sometimes has tantrums. I fetch a neighbour over, just to watch them while I go round to my mother's just to calm down. It's like she's the mother and I'm the child really. She'll throw things round the room.

● ● ●

A 15-year-old girl had a very stormy relationship with her mother. Her mother had a boyfriend and the family had recently moved to a new area. The girl's friends were older than her, and her mother disapproved. The girl had experimented with drink and drugs. The mother had a tempestuous relationship with her own mother, who had shared in the upbringing of her daughter. She was jealous of her mother's influence over her daughter and felt undermined by it. Every so often the mother 'washed her hands of her daughter', who then went to stay with her grandmother:

It went on for ages where she was just rebellious, really bad . . . One time she went out, I don't know what happened but she came back drunk. I told her off about it, sent her upstairs, and she decided she wasn't having it, so instead of going upstairs she went through the kitchen and out through the back door. So I went down to the entrance to try and stop her, and I ended up on my bonnet. Honestly, she punched me. And I was trying to get her in the house and I couldn't get her in, and all the other kids were there and they were shouting: 'Stop, stop'. I just lost control of her.

My sister came round and she diffused the situation. I went round to my other sister's for a while, and while I was there my daughter decided to take an overdose. By this time I was out of it. My sister and boyfriend sort of took over. She stayed in hospital for a few days and I didn't bother going to see her. I thought that was it, type of thing. The relationship between me and her was really up and down at the time.

● ●

Children in families with multiple problems

The largest sub-category of children in need through family stress (12 children) were children in families with multiple problems. All were aged over 7 years and all but one were boys. The children had a range of behavioural and educational problems, including violent, destructive and defiant behaviour; theft, arson, vandalism, substance abuse; and bullying, particularly of younger siblings. Families under stress experienced multiple problems, including:

- marital breakdown;
- reconstituted family;
- moving house;
- relationship breakdown;
- inadequate parenting;
- bullying;
- domestic violence; and
- ill health.

The following case studies illustrate multiple-problem situations of families under stress:

● ●

A 9-year-old boy was one of three children aged 5–9 years. His single mother was having considerable difficulty in controlling her children and problems were escalating. The mother was suffering from depression and was ineffective in disciplining her children. She was not very effective domestically and also had financial problems. The family had a long welfare history stretching back over five years.

The boy was having educational problems and would not concentrate at school. He was said to be extremely intelligent but was receiving input from a variety of sources, such as education welfare and behaviour therapists at school. He would not listen to anybody, and there was a great deal of arguing between the three boys, who were generally unchecked and uncontrolled. For example, they regularly watched adult videos. The mother said: 'They just won't listen to me. They wind each other up.' About the boy, she commented:

> He does tell lies, but I can usually tell when he's lying. He ran away once. He goes to meet older boys instead of going to school.

● ● ●

An 11-year-old boy had experienced considerable behavioural problems, such as aggressive behaviour, since his parents' marriage had broken up. His mother commented: 'He never really accepted that me and his dad had split up and he had great difficulties in accepting the new situation.'

He displayed constant dislike of the new stepfather, who was rather authoritarian and aimed to take over the role of the father completely, including the children taking his name, in spite of the fact that they still had frequent contact with their birth father. The boy's dislike of his stepfather took various forms:

> He used to be really aggressive and throw tantrums. He used to make false allegations about me all over the place, to neighbours, to friends, at school . . . He used to put salt in my tea.

The stepfather had been involved in a child protection investigation concerning some neighbour's children just prior to the period of the study. The stepfather had spent a great deal of his own life in care. The boy had regular contact with his birth father, who had remarried. The boy's mother made allegations about the new wife, for example that she was 'an alcoholic'. The new marital situation was unstable, and there was domestic violence: 'We started going out about 18 months ago and then we've been married a year now. He hit me and I left him.' Recently, the family had moved and the mother had treatment for cancer.

The boy had no educational difficulties, although he was bullied. His stepfather commented: 'He brought this upon himself because he tells on people.'

● ●

Offending behaviour

Six children were displaying behaviour that had warranted the involvement of the police. As the previous discussion has shown, children in various categories of need were involved in criminal activities, but their offending behaviour was not reported as their most significant problem. Six families reported the offending behaviour of one child as the most significant problem within the family. Their children were involved in criminal behaviour such as arson, criminal damage and burglary. Although they were also displaying behavioural problems within the home, they were classified as being in need through offending behaviour. A case study illustrates a situation of need through offending behaviour:

An 8-year-old boy lived with his 7-year-old sister and his mother and father. His father had serious alcohol misuse problems and was in prison for attempting to kill his wife. The children were on the Child Protection Register. The boy had a number of problems: violent and aggressive at school and out of control at home. He was rarely in the family home but was more often out with 'his mates', who were generally a lot older. His mother said:

> I can't keep him under control. He always likes to be out and he gets into trouble when he is there. He's always playing with older kids. He has a mind of an 18-year-old. He keeps bringing the police round to my door. Last week he was with some older lads who went and burgled an empty house and stole a bottle of whisky. Then he lit a fire in the graveyard. He has a name for himself round here. He is a young tearaway. I can't punish him – he has tantrums. He is deliberately disruptive and he gets his own way. He is very aggressive at school as well, and the teachers are very concerned about his violence.

Social deprivation

There were 25 families with children in need through social deprivation. These families were more likely to approach Social Services on their own initiative than to be referred from a professional source.

Just over a quarter of families in the study approached Social Services principally because of children in need through problems of social deprivation, poverty, or social disadvantage. Problems were of two types: specific and multiple.

Specific problems

Seven families, five of whom had no previous contact with Social Services, had specific problems associated with social deprivation; in all other aspects the families were functioning well, although in many cases there were a number of other problems, the most common being physical ill health. The majority of families had housing problems (five cases). These were of two types:

- ◆ financial, such as rent arrears, lack of funds for heating bills, carpets, etc.; and
- ◆ inadequate accommodation – substandard or overcrowded living conditions.

Multiple problems

Eighteen families in the study approached Social Services because their children were in need through multiple problems associated with social deprivation, ranging from mildly problematic to severe. Only five families had no previous contact with Social Services, whereas ten families had previously had contact on several occasions. Reasons for previous contact were varied, including child protection concerns, requests for financial assistance, parenting and health problems.

The majority of families wanted support from an allocated social worker for various problems. Some problems were often perceived by families to be *acute* and to require immediate action. Examples included refugee families living in very impoverished and overcrowded conditions and a mixed race family experiencing serious racial hatred and needing to move away from the area where they lived.

Other problems were often more long-term or *chronic*, possibly requiring intervention but not necessarily on a crisis basis. Examples included: parents experiencing depression, problem drinking, health problems, isolation, lack of support, low income and/or poor money management, more than one young child (under 5 years) and parenting problems. A case study illustrates multiple problems in socially deprived families:

● ●

A teenager was cared for by her grandmother after the death of her mother. The teenager was becoming unmanageable. The grandmother had ostensibly approached Social Services complaining about the lack of financial support she was entitled to when she was looking after a teenager in an informal fostering arrangement, but it soon became clear that a main concern was the generation gap. In addition, the girl's presence had caused problems in the grandmother's marriage.

● ● ●

The mother of a young child was having difficulty making ends meet and needed help with her finances and general support. She described her situation:
> I went to Social Services when the DSS wouldn't help and I hadn't got enough money. My son's also very active and I needed to get him into a nursery, and I was suffering from depression. I was also having problems with my daughter. You see, basically everything really.

I've had lots of financial concerns since the break up of the relationship with the father really. I was getting lots of debts. They're taking a lot off my social security at the moment. I'm only getting £49 a week . . . You don't live. You exist. I got paid yesterday and there's barely anything left and I haven't been shopping yet . . .

I'm having a lot of problems with contact with the father because he's not bringing him back when he should . . . The boy can be a handful at times. I haven't got the patience really. He's always on the go all the time. He's only just started going to bed for the last couple of months. He wouldn't go to bed at all. I was having to wait for him to fall asleep down here and then have to carry him up.

• •

Summary

Needs arose from a particular child or from family circumstances that affected a particular child. These needs fell into the categories of intrinsic need, need because of parental illness, need because of family stress, need because of offending behaviour and need because of social deprivation.

There were more boys than girls in the study, and the boys were more likely to have needs associated with offending behaviour and family stress than were the girls. The girls' needs were greater in relation to social deprivation.

Young children up to 6 years were likely to have needs arising from family stress, parental ill health and social deprivation; children in their middle years (7–12) from family stress and social deprivation; older children (13–16 years) from offending behaviour, family stress and social deprivation.

Intrinsic needs were of three types: multiple, educational and physical health.

Parental ill health needs were chronic and acute, both mental and physical, and affected children under 12 years of age in two ways: lack of parental care and the responsibilities of being young carers.

Family stress needs were long- or short-term or situation-specific and were of five main types: young mothers at crisis point; conflict because of parental disagreement; conflict caused by reconstitution of the family; families with children with behavioural problems; and children in families with multiple problems.

Offending behaviour included arson, criminal damage and burglary.

Social deprivation needs were of two types: specific concerns or multiple concerns. There was a very high self-referral rate.

Generally, there were two types of problems: acute and chronic. Acute problems often required a rapid but short-term social work response, which might include referral elsewhere. Chronic problems required longer-term social work support alongside the input of other agencies.

5 *Approaching Social Services*

The issue of access to services is central to the provision of services for children in need. The complexity of access was highlighted in the earlier national study of children in need by Aldgate and Tunstill (1995) and by the Audit Commission (1994). Access can be a problem for both children and parents.

The study parents

Parents could approach Social Services directly or indirectly. Directly, parents and families could get in touch by telephone or in person. Indirectly, they could be referred by a department within the local authority, by health professionals, by the police or by other agencies in the public and voluntary sector. Referrals could also come from anonymous sources. In 16 cases in the study, both direct and indirect methods of approach occurred.

Table 5.1 shows that more than half of the parents in the study took the initiative themselves, or a member of their family did so on their behalf. In spite of any reservations they might have had, these parents strongly saw Social Services as an agency of first resort. In five cases, relatives had made the referral, generally because of parenting problems or problems of social deprivation. For example, an anxious grandmother was worried about the care her daughter was providing for her children at a time when she was stressed by relationship problems. In another case, a woman who had been a target of her nephew's behavioural problems made the referral.

Cases involving offending behaviour were mostly referred by the families themselves; the police being involved in intrinsic problems and situations of family stress. Families of children in need for reasons of social deprivation and family stress were apparently unlikely to have professional support in approaching Social Services. Eighty-eight per cent of families experiencing social deprivation referred themselves, as did 72% of families under stress.

Table 5.1 *Sources of referral in relation to category of need*

Source of referral	Category of need					
	Intrinsic	**Parental ill health**	**Family stress**	**Offending behaviour**	**Social deprivation**	**Total**
	n=13	n=13	n=36	n=6	n=25	n=93
Family/self	8	4	26	6	22	66
Health service	3	6	7	–	3	19
Education	4	–	2	1	1	8
Police	1	–	2	–	–	3
Social work team	1	3	3	–	–	7
Housing department	1	–	–	–	1	2
Voluntary agency	1	1	–	–	–	2
Other	–	1	–	–	1	2
Total	**19**	**15**	**40**	**7**	**28**	**109**

Families with health problems were least likely to refer themselves. Among professionals, health visitors were a frequent source of referrals, particularly in cases where problems were related to intrinsic need or to parental illness and family stress. This reflected the continuing importance of health visitors in the detection and monitoring of family problems.

A minority of families were referred by education services. There are two possible reasons for this low referral rate. Firstly, in some of the study authorities, Social Services were perceived primarily as a child protection agency; therefore, only in the most extreme cases, where there were serious concerns about safeguarding children, would Education refer children to Social Services.

Secondly, children's problems, rather than being viewed holistically, may be 'departmentalised', so that behavioural problems at home are treated separately from educational problems. Parents said, for example, that they had asked the school to 'do something' about their children's behaviour at home, but schools had been reluctant to take any action if the children's behaviour at school was not a problem.

Social workers in other social work teams – for example, those based in hospitals – accounted for about 7% of referrals. These concerned families with young children, and generally in circumstances where a parent had had an accident and required short-term support.

Table 5.2 shows the distribution of referrals from different sources according to the children's age groups. Health service referrals were predominantly in the lower age group. Social work team referrals from community care teams and hospitals were similar for younger and middle-year children. Of the education service referrals, 88% concerned children in the middle years but only 12% of the children in the older age group.

Table 5.2 *Sources of referral in relation to the children's age groups*

Source of referral	Children's age groups			
	0–6	7–12	13–16	Total
Family	10	38	18	66
Health service	12	7	–	19
Education	–	7	1	8
Police	–	–	3	3
Social work teams	3	3	1	7
Housing department	–	2	–	2
Voluntary agency	1	1	–	2
Other	1	–	1	2
Total	**27**	**58**	**24**	**109**

n=93

Access to Social Services

In practical terms, access to Social Services varied. Some parents in the study found it quite easy to get in touch with Social Services. Comments included: 'Very easy – they were just on the end of a 'phone'; 'I just walked in!'

However, in spite of seeing Social Services as a positive port of call, there could be difficulties in gathering enough courage to ask for help: 'It was hard from an emotional point of view. I couldn't have done it on my own.'

Accessibility can be viewed along several dimensions: location; reception; communication; and information.

Location

Some offices were located in the middle of, or close to, the housing estates they served. Others were situated in town centres, convenient for urban but not for rural users. Some offices were clearly signposted as Social Services. Others were described as difficult to find.

Reception

Once inside, potential clients frequently found the reception area unwelcoming and had difficulty in communicating with staff through glass screens. No doubt in place for security purposes, nevertheless these measures transmitted signals of stigma to families ambivalent about using such services. By contrast, there were social services offices in the study that were friendly, open, well decorated and conveyed a real sense of welcome and reassurance.

Communication

There were two potential problem areas in communication between Social Services and families:

- the families having to repeat information to different people; and

- the families' understanding of information given to them by social workers.

Repetition of information arose from two sources: lack of continuity of service and difficulty in accessing the appropriate people. Comments were made such as:

> You can never get the same person. I find that very off-putting because somebody comes out and you see them and you know who they are. And you ring up and try to speak to them and you get given to somebody else and you have to go through it all again. You think: you don't need this.

A further obstacle to accessing services is the duty system. Being 'on duty' is perceived as stressful by social workers, and usually there is a rotational system in place. However, one social services office in the study had a social worker who spent her entire time on duty, and this was reflected in the positive comments of families, who felt that they had a named person to whom they could relate. It also meant that the duty worker was likely to remember particular referrals more quickly than a social worker who was divided between duty work and casework.

Problems surrounding the duty system may be exacerbated by the record-keeping system. Many offices had elaborate administrative processes for the filing of cases, and the retrieval of a case could take days or even weeks. If a family telephoned or called in during the retrieval period, it was likely that, in the absence of files, information had to be repeated.

With regard to understanding what was said, comments such as 'They talked to me, but it was a load of jargon' contrasted with others that were more favourable: 'They came round and explained everything.'

Information

The information available about services to families also varied. In one social services' reception area there was a rack of service leaflets in several different languages, available for families to read while they were waiting. In others, there were posters on the walls giving information on local services and helplines.

Absence of information had several implications for the families in the study. Firstly, it meant they experienced a sense of powerlessness in their early contact with Social Services. Secondly, they were disqualified from making any informed choice about what might help. Thirdly, the social workers would have been helped by the ability of the families to indicate the possible relevance of services on offer. Overall, it made the task of matching services to needs more difficult for everyone concerned.

Previous experience of Social Services

Previous experience of Social Services varied. There was no particular association between the circumstances and the reason for referral in previous and current contact. Two-thirds of the families had been in touch with Social Services before the present referral. Looking at current and previous reasons for contact with Social Services, it is evident that future problems involving Social Services were not directly predictable from previous contacts. Families experience a range of problems. At different times, different problems become more prominent.

The needs categories and previous experience

The majority of the 13 families in the intrinsic needs category who were experiencing parenting problems had already been in touch for the same reason. Another quarter of this group of families had been in contact with Social Services because of concerns over child protection. Other concerns included family conflict, parental health and social deprivation.

Just under half of the families where parental ill health was the main problem had previous contact with Social Services for various reasons, including child protection concerns and child behaviour problems. By contrast, three-quarters of the 'family stress' needs category had previous contact with Social Services for various reasons, including family conflict, child protection, parenting problems and social deprivation.

Four of the six families who were in contact because of juvenile crime had previously been in contact with Social Services for various reasons, including family conflict, parenting problems, lack of finances and child protection concerns.

More than half of the 25 families in the study who were experiencing problems of social deprivation had already been in touch for the same reason. A quarter of this group had previous contact for concerns over child protection. Other previous concerns included problems of family conflict and parenting problems, particularly where the parents themselves had been in care.

The relationship between previous contact and the type of referral

Previous contact was not associated with the current reason for referral. Of those without previous experience of Social Services, just over half made contact without professional referral. Slightly more of those with previous experience were referred, but differences were negligible.

In particular, families who came to Social Services with parenting problems were likely to have had prolonged previous contact. They were mostly parents of young families who had at least one child under the age of three, and they were finding that life in general 'was getting on top of them', with the behaviour of the child designated as 'in need' being the final straw. All were single mothers who had serious health problems and were in conflict with ex-partners. Thus they represented a group of families who were under extreme stress during the first few years of their child's lives.

Expectations of Social Services

The expectations that parents had when they came to Social Services were influenced by three main factors:

- ♦ concerns over the implications of contact with Social Services;
- ♦ previous experience of Social Services; and
- ♦ perceptions of the role of Social Services.

Concerns over the implications of contact with Social Services

In spite of seeing Social Services as an agency of first resort, just under half of the families explicitly expressed concerns over contact with Social Services. Families had several fears.

Stigma

Stigma is a perennial theme in the delivery of welfare services, and it is to be expected that it will feature in the views of potential recipients of Social Services. However, this study found that more than three-quarters of the parents were unconcerned about stigma, and indeed saw Social Services as a positive helping agency. The remaining quarter were concerned that they would be stigmatised in the local community by contact with Social Services or would be an embarrassment to their families. Comments ranged from 'I hoped no one I knew would see me going into the department' to 'My sister said: "What on earth would the family think?"'

More parents who had previously been in contact with Social Services, either once or on several occasions, were worried about stigma than was the case for those with no previous contact. More parents of younger children were worried about stigma than parents of children in the middle years. There was even less likelihood of concern among parents of older children.

Worries about children being 'taken away'

Parents worried that their children could be taken away by Social Services. This was the most frequent concern. Parents who had not previously had contact with Social Services were more likely to be worried than those who had been in contact on one or more occasion(s). Parents of young children were most anxious about the powers of Social Services and frequently cited the power of social workers 'to get their children adopted'. Professionally referred parents were more anxious than the non-professionally referred, because they felt there was less control over their association with Social Services. A mother who was having difficulty in managing her 6-year-old daughter commented: 'I was a bit worried at first. I was afraid that they would see that the problem was that the mother couldn't cope and they would have to take the children away and get them adopted.'

A mother suffering from post-natal depression said: 'I thought that they might take my baby off me. I know people are always looking for babies to adopt. They might think I was mentally unfit to be a parent.' And a mother with severe financial problems said: 'It's my biggest worry that they're going to take the children away.'

Misinterpretation of family circumstances

A minority of parents were concerned that Social Services would misinterpret or make too much of their situation, possibly labelling them as inadequate parents. One mother commented that: 'People have been accused of doing things they haven't.' This fear was just as common among those who had previously been in touch with Social Services as among new service users and was equally prevalent across the needs categories. Younger parents were more worried than the older ones.

The effects of previous experience on current approaches

Families in all categories of need had had both good and bad experiences of Social Services in the past. Some felt negative about Social Services as a whole; others had negative feelings about individual social workers. Despite their reservations families continued to turn to Social Services for help.

Previous contact with Social Services influenced, for good or for bad, what Social Services could offer. For example, a mother who had previously succeeded in obtaining day care for her daughter through Social Services approached them optimistically on a second occasion. Another parent who had a good service from the hospital social worker was disappointed when, after she left hospital, she failed to obtain services from her local social worker.

There were a small number of parents who, as children, had been in care for various reasons, including adoption breakdown and child abuse. The fears of these parents were acute because of their own experiences, although they could also see Social Services as a source of help.

Some families had had previous contact on child protection issues. Few of these families seemed to regard Social Services with resentment or fear. In most cases in the study, the allegations against the family were unfounded, according to the families' reports. This finding has resonance with the findings of studies on child protection, where families were able to understand the difficulty of the social worker's role and appreciate when a difficult job had been well done (Sharland et al. 1996).

The children's involvement in approaching Social Services

Given that one of the principles of the Children Act 1989 is the need to consult children about their wishes and feelings, children in this study were asked how they felt about their families' involvement with Social Services. Forty-one children from the age of 7 and upwards were interviewed, and more than half felt that their parents had involved them in approaching Social Services. Children in need through family stress were more likely to be involved than those in need through offending behaviour or social deprivation. In cases of offending behaviour, parents took the initiative to have Social Services 'sort out' their children; in social deprivation cases, parents felt it was inappropriate to share their financial worries with their children.

Although the majority of children were in their middle or adolescent years, they were not always aware of the circumstances surrounding their contact with Social Services. Just over half of the children knew by whom they had been referred to Social Services. All the children with intrinsic needs (mostly children in their middle years) knew by whom they had been referred; this was the case for roughly half of the children in the other categories of need.

Only one-third of the children interviewed knew why their families were in contact with Social Services. It was difficult to ascertain why this was the case. Children could have opted out, or they could have been left out of the process of approaching Social Services by design or unwittingly. It could be that, in families with a multiplicity of problems, children were unclear which problem or problems had led to the referral.

The children's views on their families' problems

The children's views on the nature of their families' problems were explored. Their comments suggest that they were sensitive to the plethora of problems faced by themselves and their families. They were also concerned about the impact of family problems on themselves. School was a source of worry, and the children were anxious that they were not achieving as well as they might. School was also full of challenges in peer relationships. The following quotes give a picture of the range of children's perceptions:

> I know my mum is having a really difficult time; and it would be great if someone could help her . . . she isn't very well a lot of the time. I worry at school about her and I can't do me sums.

Parents try and pretend that everything is OK, even if they aren't – and I know they aren't – and I can't help Mum and Dad as much as I want, but I try.

I hate going school. I'm always in trouble. See, me mum can't get me the football kit and Mr Wright tells me off. I get teased because I don't have my kit. My mum says she'll ask Social Services to sort me some kit.

My brother and I watch the lottery and we reckon it would stop our mum being so worried about all the things, not just the money stuff.

I can't handle them splitting up; it makes me want to do mad things; last week I got really mad and nutted a bloke . . . me dad thinks the Social Services will make me OK, but they don't understand.

School is OK; I quite like it and I like the geography teacher, but I do stupid things at school when things are worse at home.

My mum's gone to Social Services to get me some shoes; I hope they'll be Nike.

I hate it when me mam and John fight. I just go to my room and read my comics. I wish he would go away.

What the children hoped for

The study revealed that children had a general grasp of what was going on in their families and often knew more than their parents realised about family tensions and what lay behind them. When it came to understanding what Social Services might offer, a sophisticated perception was understandably beyond their knowledge. They did, however, indicate the importance of help – financial help and someone for their parents to talk to. A minority were concerned that Social Services might take them away from their families. One child had a friend who was a foster child. Another knew a child who had been adopted.

Children hoped parental conflict would be resolved. Some, under consider-able stress at home, thought that a break from their families might be helpful. Children in need through social deprivation hoped that Social Services would give the family money, but also hoped that life would be less stressful for them and their parents.

Overall, the children interviewed gave accounts of their lives which showed that they were party to the troubles of their families to a lesser or greater degree. Whilst children's ages obviously influenced their perceptions, it was clear that parenting styles played their part in whether children were involved in the contact with Social Services or not. Some parents had included children only to the extent that they told them they were going to ask Social Services to 'sort them out'. Others, especially those in the role of young carers, were very much part of the discussions on the problems. Overall, children were not really knowledgeable about how services might help them. Some said explicitly that this was the province of their parents.

Summary

The majority of families who referred themselves to Social Services saw Social Services as a helping agency of first resort. Some families who were referred by others also share this view. Others were not so sure.

Ease of access to Social Services varied. A positive experience in the access procedure was associated with a positive experience in the rest of the contact with Social Services.

Inefficient record retrieval caused families to have to repeat their narratives to several individuals. The duty system generally militated against continuity on the part of workers who delivered services.

Expectations were influenced by concern over the implications of contact, previous experience of Social Services and perceptions about the role of Social Services.

Particular areas of anxiety in approaching Social Services related to the stigma of contacting Social Services, the fears of children being taken away and the fears of misinterpretation.

Children were sensitive to the needs of their parents and themselves but had less understanding of the role of Social Services.

6

The families and Social Services: the wish-list

Expectations of the service response

This chapter explores the outcomes that families wanted to derive from their contact with Social Services. Both in terms of the legislative framework and in the views of the public, 'social services' includes the provision of practical and material resources and a professional service provided by social workers. It is sometimes more difficult for potential service users, unfamiliar with Social Services, to have a clear image in their minds of what constitutes *social work* as opposed to what constitutes a *social service*.

Social work activity can take the form of explicit and identifiable direct work with children and their families, or it may consist in working with staff in other organisations on their behalf. Direct work may include assessment, planning, casework and the provision of practical services. Indirect work may involve planning, advocacy and liaison with other agencies (see, for example, Compton and Galloway 1989).

Parents anticipated various benefits from their contact with Social Services and had relatively clear ideas about what might help them at the point they approached Social Services. Table 6.1 indicates the main outcomes they anticipated.

Table 6.1 *Outcomes anticipated by the parents*

Anticipated outcome	Number of cases
Support/advocacy	66
Help with child development	40
Improvement in family relationships	39
Alleviation of practical problems	28

n=>93 because categories are not mutually exclusive

Support/advocacy

Two-thirds of the parents felt that they needed support through talking over their problems with someone. Families who were experiencing problems with their children's behaviour felt that they needed someone who would give them support and advice when they needed it. This is illustrated by the comments of a mother who was having severe difficulties coping with her teenage daughter:

> I think sometimes it's nice to know there's somebody out there that is completely separate from your family, to come in and sort of diffuse the [situation] . . . to give you advice on . . . not how to bring them up or anything like that but how to cope with certain situations.

It was anticipated that discussion would not only relieve stress but would also contribute to problem-solving: 'to talk to someone outside the family, to get my head into perspective'. Discussion with a neutral but experienced person would be constructive:

> I need another string to my bow which might help my anxiety about the future and my ability to care for the children.

Parents who wanted someone they could talk to or who could befriend them were generally coping with a number of overwhelming difficulties, including child behaviour problems and social deprivation.

In cases where parents were having to cope with aggressive or difficult behaviour, they were concerned about the consequences if they suddenly lost control. They felt that it would alleviate their responsibility if someone else knew about the situation:

> If everything suddenly went wrong, and anything happened, then the Social Services would know the situation and would know that it was nothing that I was doing which is causing the situation, and I would be covered if things went too far. My back would also be covered if someone else reported the situation.

Parents were not trying to shed responsibility for their children and their problems but were rather looking for support in the hope of being able to continue to cope: 'I felt that I was at breaking point. That was why I asked. I don't ask for help easily.'

Those parents who were having difficulties with an ex-partner wanted help and support when they had to deal with other people, for example when there were concerns about the way in which the ex-partner was looking after the children or affecting the children's well-being.

One father was concerned about the contact his 8-year-old son was having with his mother, who had a history of alcoholism and violence. He said that he had turned to Social Services because he thought it helped to 'have someone a bit stronger on your case . . . an official body working for you'.

Social workers were viewed as 'an unattached third person in an emotional situation' and as providing 'a professional angle in an essentially personal and emotional manner'.

Help with the children's development

Two-fifths of the parents in the study felt that contact with Social Services would help their child's development. They anticipated benefits from Social Services in a number of ways:

♦   direct intervention in their children's behaviour;

♦   advice on parenting techniques in order to help them address their children's development themselves;

♦   the opportunity for their children to mix socially outside the family; and

♦   to obtain space for carers and children.

Twenty-seven parents who were having problems with their children were hoping for some way of 'getting through' to their children and improving their behaviour. Parents hoped that problems could be expertly diagnosed – 'to find out what is wrong with my child' – and that solutions would be offered by the professionals.

Sometimes families hoped to use the authority role of Social Services to control their children. Three families talked in terms of wanting to 'teach their children a lesson'. In two of these cases the parents had suffered escalating behavioural problems with one of their children for many years, and this had culminated in offending behaviour. They wanted Social Services to 'put their child into care for a short time', in order to provide the equivalent of the 'short, sharp shock':

> I wanted to teach the boys a lesson, because they were being naughty, let
> them know what could happen if they came into contact with Social Services.

Parents with concerns about their children's schooling hoped that, through liaison with the school and the education authority, the social workers could influence schools to take more account of their children's needs: 'She needs somebody else to bring her out of herself, to stop the phobia recurring all the time, to find out what the problem is.'

Parents hoped that Social Services could help them to diagnose behavioural problems in their children and develop parenting skills to implement solutions: 'Someone to let me know what was going wrong and what could be done to help him'. Parents expressed this hope explicitly:

> I want someone to teach practical parenting. And: 'I wanted a flying squad at the time. I wanted any ideas, any way of leaving me, more or less, in control.

Twenty of the study children were restricted socially, either because they were too young to go to school or because the main parent had some disability. Carers hoped that Social Services would provide the opportunity for them to mix with other children for social development, for example 'to teach him to share'.

Carers with disabilities particularly regretted the effect their disability had on their children's lives. For example, one mother, seriously ill after a colostomy and often too ill to take the children on outings, wanted her 8-year-old son to go to an after-school club for the children of working mothers in order to provide activities outside the home. As the family was new to the area and was used to a rural community, she was wary of letting her son go out on his own to play. Her eldest son also needed some space to do his homework.

Parents hoped that Social Services would provide the opportunity for children to have their own space away from their parents and vice versa: 'There's times when we both need a break from each other . . . It does us both good.'

Improvement in family relationships

Two-fifths of the families in the study were hoping that the intervention of Social Services would improve family relationships. In particular, parents who were having difficulty with their children's behaviour were concerned about the negative impact not only on the well-being of other children in the family but also on the parental relationship. It was anticipated that Social Services could, by addressing the parents' ability to manage the child, improve the relationships in the family as a whole. This anticipated benefit was summed up by the carer of a 6-year-old who was defiant and aggressive: 'If she'll improve, we'll all improve.'

The problem behaviour could affect all the family. Other parents commented:

> It'll give the other children a chance . . . they have to put up with an awful lot sometimes.

> Sometimes his behaviour really gets to us . . . I have only got my husband to take it out on and I always take it out on him when he gets home.

> I wouldn't say our marriage is falling apart but it's slightly rocky ... I don't necessarily mean to be aggressive with my husband, but it seems I'm forever doing it . . . I try to say to myself, I mustn't do it, I must calm my temper, that kind of thing, but after a while I just do it anyway.

Parents were concerned that, without intervention, long-term damage would occur in their relationship with the children who were causing problems:

> It's affecting my relationship with him . . . I'm ashamed to say it, but there are times when I feel repulsed by him, when he comes to give me a hug or something like that . . . it's terrible, feeling like that with your own son, but he really does get me like that sometimes, because I never know whether he's telling me the truth or not.

Just over two-fifths of the parents wanted some space for themselves, both as respite from their children's behaviour problems and as 'time out' to ease the stresses of the daily demands of others. This might be simply to do what they themselves wanted and regain a sense of identity as an independent adult rather than as a parent or partner, to catch up on housework or to sleep:

> I said to the doctor, when I first became ill, if I could just go somewhere on my own, without the child, for a couple of days. I felt I just wanted to sleep, solidly for two days.

In particular, parents of children who had a variety of problems, such as ill health, social deprivation and relations with parents, longed for some time out for themselves, as they generally felt overwhelmed with problems and had little or no informal support:

> I'm on call 365 days a year, seven days a week, and I don't get a break. It's not as if I can pop round the corner to me nan or . . .

Approaches to Social Services were made in the hope of compensating for lack of an extended family:

> One of the key problems is lack of support. I would love him to have a surrogate granny, or surrogate grand-dad. I used to go up to school and I used

to see the grannies hugging the kids when they came out. When he comes out, there's nobody there for him only me.

Single parents looked for alleviation of their constant 'togetherness' with their children:

As much as I love him, we both need a break. If he had a mother, I could go out fishing or whatever.

They also looked for a break from their constant lone responsibility for their children:

If their father was someone to hand the children to at the weekends it would help both of us. It would help me to be a better parent.

Couples, too, hoped for time away from their children. For example, two parents who were experiencing aggressive and dangerous behaviour from their 8-year-old son were desperate for some kind of respite care, saying that they needed: 'someone to take him off our hands for a weekend at a time. We can get on with our lives for that bit of time.' A parent who was experiencing violent and aggressive behaviour from a 13-year-old child said:

He winds me up. It has a terrible effect on me . . . it was times like that when I needed to tell someone can you take him away.

Alleviation of a practical problem or specific need

Just over a quarter of parents in the study hoped that Social Services would provide immediate practical help, either as the only service required or in conjunction with other, ongoing services. The former situation, in which the provision of the service would remove the specific need, was illustrated by a family who had moved house and, having no carpet for the new house, went to Social Services to obtain funding.

In the latter situation, the provision of a practical service could substantially reduce stress within the family. The provision of emergency money for heating or food would have an immediate impact. Parents who had health problems also felt that Social Services would access practical services on their behalf, such as bath aids and supplies of materials for incontinence problems, articles that had not been forthcoming from health services.

The parents' perceptions of services that could meet their needs

The services parents felt would meet their needs were of three main types (see also Table 6.2):

♦ **social work support** – a flexible combination of social, interpersonal and practical interventions based on professional knowledge;

♦ **child- and family-centred services** – community care, accommodation, respite care, activities, day care (abbreviated in Table 6.2 as 'cfc'); and

♦ **other services** – housing, Section 17 money, help with health services, help with education (abbreviated in Table 6.2 as 'other').

Some parents were active in seeking specific solutions to their problems: seeking help from Social Services was one form of problem-solving activity. Others had not determined in their own mind what kind of services would help them; they just knew that they needed 'help'. This group also included three families who came into contact with Social Services reluctantly and did not particularly want a service at all.

Table 6.2 *Services wanted by parents, according to category of need*

Services wanted	Category of need					
	Intrinsic	Parental ill health	Family stress	Offending behaviour	Social deprivation	Total
Community care (cfc)	–	7	1	–	–	8
Social work support	11	7	35	5	13	71
Section 17 money (other)	–	–	–	1	15	16
Housing (other)	2	1	2	–	9	14
Help with health services (other)	6	4	7	–	–	17
Help with education (other)	5	–	2	1	1	9
Accommodation (cfc)	3	–	3	1	–	7
Respite care (cfc)	1	3	5	1	1	11
Day care (cfc)	–	3	3	1	5	12
Activities (cfc)	4	1	2	1	–	8
Total services wanted	**32**	**26**	**60**	**11**	**44**	**173**

Social work support

The most requested form of help was social work support. As discussed above, this was generally, but not invariably, viewed as being a means to an end and not simply as 'talking'. Moreover, contact with a social worker was frequently seen as necessary, either to access other services for which social workers were gatekeepers or to gain knowledge of other services available. The opportunity to discuss problems with a neutral expert was also valued.

Social work support was viewed as particularly helpful where problems were generated by family stress. Additionally, just over half of the parents with problems of parental ill health thought social work support would be helpful.

Child- and family-centred services

One-third of the parents in the study wanted child- and family-centred services such as day care and sporting or club activities, respite care, accommodation and support for themselves from adult community care teams. More parents of children who were in the middle-age group wanted child- and family-related services than parents of younger or older children. Parents of children with intrinsic needs and parental ill health needs were more likely to want this type of service. About a third of the parents of children in need through family stress or offending behaviour wanted this type of services in contrast to only a fifth of the parents of children in need through social deprivation.

Requests for these services varied between those families who had problems that were mainly *child-centred*, such as families in the intrinsic and offending behaviour categories of need, and those with more *family-centred* problems, such as families in the parental illness or social deprivation categories.

Parents experienced children's behavioural problems with varying degrees of severity. The behaviour could vary from mere defiance and 'backchat', to violence, aggression and criminal behaviour. Parents' requests for help were of two types:

- ◆ advice and techniques for disciplining their children in difficult but not desperate situations; and

- ◆ social work action to resolve their problems in situations of severe distress.

As an illustration of the first type of request for help, a parent said that she wanted the social worker to 'advise me in what to do to find out the problem so I can do something about it'. Another wanted 'someone to let me know what was going wrong and what could be done to help him'. As an example of the second type of request, a parent said that she wanted 'something doing about his bloody behaviour; his violence and vandalism'.

There were 14 families in contact with Social Services because of parental illness or deprivation who wanted general support, day or respite care and, in one case, an after-school club. Their situations included problems such as post-natal depression, in which case parents wanted a break and some emotional support. Two parents needed to make arrangements for the care of their children while they were in hospital.

Five parents were having problems with their children following a relationship breakdown with their partners, because the loss and turmoil of separation had temporarily inhibited their parenting capacities. These families were also overwhelmed by a number of difficulties, such as poverty, ill health and social isolation.

One parent was suffering from post-natal depression after the birth of her only son, and was also distressed because her husband had left her. She said of her approach to Social Services:

> I was expecting someone to come along and make it all better. When you feel like that, you do feel that somebody has got a magic wand. I don't know what I wanted. I didn't know whether I was coming or going.

There were two types of need for respite care: crisis situation and planned care.

Crisis situation

Seven parents in the study wanted respite care because they were in a state of desperation, having 'reached the end of their tether'. Five parents were having serious problems with the behaviour of one of their children (all but one were boys), mainly in the context of family stress but also, to a lesser degree, in cases of intrinsic needs or offending behaviour.

The children were violent, aggressive and destructive, often in a situation where younger siblings were being negatively affected. In these cases, respite care was frequently requested alongside social work support. Parents did not always have any clear idea about what they wanted out of the respite care except immediate relief from stress.

Planned care

Four parents wanted respite care on a longer, planned basis. Two had needs relating to parental illness and were putting in place arrangements for the care of their children in the event of hospitalisation and, in one case, of eventual death.

Seven parents of children with serious behavioural problems wanted their child to be accommodated. These children tended to be older: five were over 12 and two over six. Six of the seven were boys. Like those who wanted respite care, these had 'reached the end of their tether' with their children. Three of these families were in contact because of intrinsic needs, three because of family stress and one because of offending behaviour.

Until they approached Social Services, some parents were unaware of respite care and thought that accommodation was the only solution:

> We came to the conclusion that the only thing available was for the child to go into care.

Motivation for requests for accommodation varied in emphasis from a need to help the *child* and a need to help the *parent*.

Need to help the child. A case study serves to illustrate this category:

> A case of intrinsic need concerned a 15-year-old boy who had developed drug-induced psychosis and at the time of the study was in an adult psychiatric hospital. His parents approached Social Services for help in obtaining for him child-centred accommodation that was more suited to his needs.

Need to help the parent. Some families were at the end of their tether. A case study serves to illustrate this category:

> A 13-year-old girl from the north of England moved to the south with her mother and her mother's new partner, whom she found it difficult to accept. Her behaviour became unmanageable. She was abusive and in trouble with the police for shoplifting. Her mother despaired and wanted the child to go into care.

At the same time, there were a number of families who expressly said that they did not want their children to 'go into care'. Despite the children's severe behavioural problems, the parents were concerned that damage would occur to the family structure and that the children would experience feelings of rejection.

Combining family- and child-centred help

There were eight parents in the study who wanted some kind of activities to occupy their children after school or during the holidays. The children were all aged 7–12 and all but one were boys. The parents wanted a break from their children's problem behaviour for their own benefit. At the same time, parents were not unaware of their children's needs and saw after-school clubs as a positive place for activities that the children could enjoy and do well at. A case study serves to illustrate this situation:

● ●

A mother whose 9-year-old daughter had severe behavioural problems said:
It's the holidays I dread . . . I can just about cope when she comes home from school . . . I'm trying to get some activities. She's got lots of things that she's really good at like sport and dancing. I wish I could get her to something like that. Then it would be something for her to shine at. She really loves acting. She likes to be the centre of attention.

● ●

A mother with a chronic complaint was hoping for club activities because she herself was not well enough to give her 8-year-old boy the attention that he needed. She hoped that the activities would both provide channels for the child's energy and relieve a stressful situation.

The 12 parents in the study who wanted under-fives' day care for their children were either living in poverty, suffering from post-natal depression or experiencing family stress and, unsurprisingly, had a number of problems. They had two main motives for requesting day care:

   ♦   for themselves, to have some time on their own, to have a break or to catch up with other chores; and

   ♦   for their child, to have a chance to mix with other children to combat their social isolation.

Other services

Just over half of the parents in the study wanted other services such as financial help or assistance with housing, education or health services. Their motivation for approaching Social Services was that they believed that the professional input would facilitate access to other services and provide a boost to a lack of confidence.

Health-related services

Seventeen parents wanted help in dealing with health-related services for themselves or for their children. They included:

- parents with physical health needs, requesting practical help such as occupational therapy or adaptations to the home;

- parents with mental health needs, for example depression, requesting help from a psychiatrist or psychologist; and

- the parents of children with serious behavioural problems, requesting help from any quarter: health, education or social services.

Education

Nine children had problems at school; for example, they were truanting or were about to be, or had been, excluded from school. Parents wanted professional support in dealing with education departments in order to help their children back into mainstream education.

Three of these children were receiving no full-time education, although one had a part-time tutor. Without schooling, the bored and disruptive children represented a full-time problem for parents, adding to existing pressures when families were already experiencing stress and social deprivation. These circumstances also had a negative effect on the children's education.

Housing

The parents wanted various kinds of help from Social Services in terms of their housing problems:

- support for housing applications – often part of the official procedure required the involvement of Social Services;

- support for housing transfer applications;

- intervention in cases of rent arrears; and

- refugee settlement.

Families who wanted help with housing were generally living in poverty, although family stress, intrinsic need and parental ill health were also associated with housing problems.

Housing problems represented the main reason for approaching Social Services in nine cases. These were mainly of three types and could occur singly or in combination:

♦ overcrowded accommodation;

♦ inappropriate accommodation; and

♦ substandard accommodation.

Eight families lived in overcrowded conditions. Imminent births would soon result in further overcrowding for three families. Housing and financial problems often went together. Overcrowding could also interact with other problems, such as the health of the children. For example, a child with epilepsy currently had to share a room with his 1-year-old sister, who would probably have been rather frightened had she witnessed an attack. Damp conditions were a problem and were often associated with negative effects on the children's health.

The children's needs derived from housing problems in various other ways. Two examples will serve to illustrate individual needs. Firstly, a child of dual heritage suffered such racial abuse that the family approached Social Services for support in a housing transfer application. Secondly, the parents of an unruly and disruptive 7-year-old boy who lived in a sixth-floor flat were terrified that their child was going to jump out of the window. They had previously found him hanging from the sill.

Financial support

There were three main categories of financial need:

♦ for essential subsistence items, such as food, clothing, electricity and nappies;

♦ for essential household items, such as cots, carpets, beds, refrigerators and cookers; and

♦ for special expenditure, such as school uniform.

Parents in the study who approached Social Services because they wanted some financial help all referred themselves. All but one family were classified as in need because of social deprivation.

Some approaches were solely for financial assistance. For example, a single mother who had just moved house and could not afford carpets for the new property was concerned about her children running around on bare floors. She hoped Social Services would approach the Charities Board on her behalf for a grant towards the cost of carpets. There were no other problems in the family that required the intervention of Social Services.

Community care

Need for community services were of two types: short-term and long-term.

Short-term help. Five parents wanted short-term help with household tasks. All had young children under school age. The parents were either suffering from post-natal depression or had been incapacitated by an accident.

Long-term help. Three parents wanted longer-term help because of chronic ill health. These families tended to be older, with children in their middle years. A couple with two children aged 8 and 11 needed some adaptations to their house because of the mother's disability. Following an eligibility assessment, a referral was made for support for the children as young carers. There were no other problems in the family.

Single or multiple services

As discussed earlier, the services wanted were of three main types:

♦ social work support;

♦ child- and family-centred services – community care, accommodation, respite care, activities, day care; and

♦ other services – housing, Section 17 money, help with health services, help with education.

In some cases, parents felt they would benefit from simultaneously receiving services of one or more types. Table 6.3 shows that multiple services were those most often requested.

Table 6.3 Types of service requested by the parents

Type of service	Number of cases
Social work support	26
Single service	16
Multiple services	51

n=93

It is significant that there was little variation across the needs categories in requests for multiple services. The bias towards wanting several services together underlines the fact that it was the serious and complex nature of the problems of the families in the study that impelled them to seek help. The findings suggest that social services departments have a very important role to play as a gateway to a range of services as well as in providing a range of services from within the social services departments themselves.

Social work support. Just over a quarter of the parents in the study approached Social Services only for social work support. Half of the parents wanting social work support had child-centred problems – cases of intrinsic need, family stress or offending behaviour. Their situations were often difficult but not necessarily desperate. They requested social work support either directly or through referrals made for them by other agencies or family members.

Single services. Sixteen families in the study wanted one particular service and generally had a clear idea of what that service should be. The parents who wanted a single service were likely to approach Social Services on their own initiative. Their children tended to be younger; seven children were under the age of 7 and a further six were aged 7–12 years. It was obvious that financial support was the most prevalent reason for a request for a single service. Families could receive one-off financial emergency assistance without further recourse to Social Services. Similarly, in the pursuit of housing support, the involvement of Social Services was more or less standard practice and did not imply the need for any further assistance.

Multiple services. Over half of the families (55%) who approached Social Services wanted a combination of services, often with social work support as part of the package. The families who wanted a package of services had a range of family problems, including extreme poverty, poor housing, social isolation and depression, and an inability to cope with both younger and older children in the family.

The prevalence of requests for combined services varied according to the needs categories; most requests related to the intrinsic need cases, followed by parental ill health, family stress, offending behaviour and social deprivation. The parents wanted four main combinations of services:

 ♦   social work support plus practical help;

 ♦   social work support plus *child and family* services;

- social work support plus help with access to *other* services; and

- a combination of all three of the above.

The children's wish-list

Although some of the children may not have been able to appreciate the reasons for approaching Social Services, they seemed to be aware of the types of services wanted and what they hoped these services would achieve. Table 6.4 shows that the services wanted by most children were general support (18 cases) and help with schooling (7 cases).

Table 6.4 *The children's wish-list for services*

Services wanted	Number
Housing/money	2
Health-related	1
General support	18
Accommodation	1
Respite care	2
Home care	1
Activities	2
Help with schooling	7
None	10

Forty-one children were interviewed; n=>41 because categories are not mutually exclusive

Notably, almost three-quarters of the children with intrinsic needs (71%) wanted general support. General support was the only service wanted by children in need through offending behaviour, although the majority of these children did not want any services.

Children were hoping to achieve a number of benefits from services besides support for themselves and their parents. Just under 40% of the children, mostly those in need through family stress, were hoping that parental conflict would be resolved. To a lesser extent, some children (17%) wanted help with their behaviour and a break from their families – all of these were children with intrinsic needs. Children in need through social deprivation hoped for support and alleviation of a practical or financial need.

Summary

Parents anticipated a range of benefits from their contacts with Social Services:

- support and advocacy;

- help with child development;

- improvement in family relationships; and

- alleviation of family problems.

It is worthy of note that almost half of the families in the study cited family relationships as a problem area with which they wanted help. Whilst this did refer in large measure to the children's behaviour, relationships with partners were also very much to the fore.

The services they felt would meet these needs were of three main types:

- social work support;

- child- and family-centred services (e.g., respite and day care); and

- other services (e.g., help with housing and Section 17 payments).

Although some parents did want short-term help, other parents felt they would appreciate support that was not time limited.

The children were aware of the types of services they and their families wanted. Although they had a limited understanding of what might be on offer, they hoped to achieve a number of benefits for themselves as well as for their parents. Just under 40% of the children were hoping that parental conflict would be resolved.

Other aspirations on the part of the children were for:

- help with their behaviour

- a break from their families; and

- alleviation of practical or financial need.

7 *The other side of the door: the families who received services*

Four examples give a flavour of the lives and problems of the families and children who received services:

● ●

I had a problem with my social security money this morning . . . yet again it wasn't in the bank . . . and I went to the bank and blew a gasket. I went into the social services office . . . and in the end she gets on the 'phone to them and of course as soon as she said the magic word, Social Services, everything's sweetness and light.

● ● ●

He [the social worker] wrote to the water board for me to stop disconnection. He was supposed to be writing to the DSS to reduce payments on my social fund loan, but I've not heard anything.

● ● ●

[The social worker] talks about how things are with the children and that . . . and gives us ideas about how to deal with them . . . he helps us to discipline them. I get a support worker. And she's found me a child-minder which will start next week, for six hours a week. Someone comes in to me two hours a week, and the personal care person comes in twice a week and she's also contacted Homestart . . . She normally does practical things . . . feeding, changing, hoovering, dusting, whatever I ask her to do . . . They offer help and support for the family, bits and pieces, whatever I ask.

● ● ●

A young mother, who had repeatedly contacted Social Services, was suffering from post-natal depression. Her husband had recently left her. On returning home, she had home care, reducing from 24 hours a day to nothing, for a period of three months, with a social worker on hand, plus help from a number of other voluntary and statutory agencies, including health and Social Services.

● ●

The rest of this chapter is divided into three parts:

♦ The first outlines the issues that brought families to Social Services and explains the factors that determined the responses they received.

♦ The second explores the relationship between the individual needs categories and the service provision. These accounts also underline the scale and complexity of the challenges facing social workers in the seven social services departments in recognising and responding to a range of children's needs. To provide a coherent framework for the descriptions of the family situations, they are explored under the five categories of need.

♦ The third reviews the range and types of services that the families received.

The issues that brought families to Social Services and the responses they received

Parents approached, or were referred to, Social Services with one of two main aspirations. They either hoped:

♦ that Social Services would help them with their needs as a family; or

♦ that Social Services would offer help in relation to one particular child.

Therefore, children *and* their families were potential recipients of the provision of social services. Services directed towards children could benefit parents and families; the alleviation of the parents' problems could benefit the children.

Service provision will be influenced by the availability of services as well as by the professional assessment of need. This is one of the dilemmas at the heart of the provision of services under Part III of the Children Act to meet the needs of children in need (see Aldgate and Tunstill 1995; Colton et al. 1993; Audit Commission 1994; Social Services Inspectorate 1997 and 1999).

The allocation of resources can be examined along several dimensions, including whether or not services are offered, the length of time over which services are provided, the nature of the services and whether families are offered single or multiple services. These aspects of service provision will now be explored, with particular reference to the categories of need.

Immediate or delayed response?

Being provided with a service or being turned down for a service represented the key outcomes of the process of approaching Social Services. The process of decision-making could be complex. An indication of the likely outcome of an application for services was usually given to families at one of the three following stages:

- ♦ at the first point of contact, by telephone or in person;

- ♦ at the assessment interview; and

- ♦ by letter or telephone from the social work office, after the assessment interview.

Two-fifths of the families (37) knew within one week of approaching Social Services what they could expect; and a further 21 knew within two weeks. However, for about a quarter of the families, the period of waiting extended into months.

There was an association between the category of need and whether families were offered services or not. Almost half of the parents in the social deprivation category were refused services. The parents of three of the six children seeking services because of offending behaviour were also turned down. By contrast, the categories most likely to obtain services were those due to parental ill health and, to a slightly lesser extent, family stress. Children with intrinsic needs were in the middle range; around two-fifths were refused.

In the cases of ill health, there were some indications that families had been referred by others rather than approaching Social Services themselves. By contrast, families who were in the categories of family stress and social deprivation were most likely to have referred themselves and were the highest category to be refused services.

It is difficult to interpret these findings because of the small numbers involved. However, it is tempting to speculate that social services departments remain less responsive to self-expressed need than to that put forward by a fellow professional. In addition, it may be that different professionals have different influences on the decision-making process. Social Services may be more willing to unequivocally accept referrals from health professionals. This may be partly because of the recognition accorded to health professionals by social workers. It may also relate to the fact that in this study, as in the earlier one on Section 17 services (Aldgate and Tunstill 1995), health and

Social Services have much more clearly defined channels of communication and co-operation. This study suggests that there is an urgent need for clear mechanisms of interagency working to be developed among all those agencies who are concerned with the welfare of children.

In addition, it is clear that far less attention is paid to the voices of families who themselves seek help directly from Social Services. If working in partnership with families is to be taken seriously, and the Children Act concept of listening to children is to be given its due status, then Social Services needs to develop a responsive approach, one that takes seriously the concerns and needs of the children and of their families.

Service provision

Overall, more than two-thirds of the families who approached or were referred to Social Services obtained a service, even if this was a single further interview.

There was an apparent relationship between being offered fewer, as opposed to more, services and being given a speedy decision. The fewer the services obtained, the quicker the decision. Half of the families who were offered one service tended to know the outcome of their assessment within a week. In general, the greater the number of services offered, the longer was the period between assessment and implementation. In a situation where two or more services were offered, only a quarter of the recipients were informed of the outcome of their assessment within a week.

There was an association between the number of services offered and the source of referral. Families who were professionally referred were more likely to receive more than one service. This may well be related to the threshold of referral by other professionals. Families are referred by other professionals only when children are clearly perceived to fit Social Services' criteria for high priority services for children in need. Conversely, even though some families who were self-referred expressed high levels of stress, this had no association with either the number or the type of services offered; nor indeed with the age of the child in need.

Variations in service provision according to category of need

Once families had succeeded in surmounting the first hurdle and been accepted for the provision of services, the study identified further variations in the response of Social Services to children within different categories of need.

The 'family stress'/needs category (the largest category in the study with 36 cases), was associated with high levels of service provision (see Table 7.1). Although fewer families who came into this category got to the point of service provision, it is clear that, once they did, social workers took account of the diverse needs manifested in a family. Consequently, these families were just as likely as families in other needs categories to obtain one, two or three services. There was evidence of careful and imaginative approaches to the provision of a range of services. However, where the problem was one of social deprivation, fewer families got into the system. When they did, they were more likely to be offered only a single service. This frequently took the form of financial help: referral to a charity or referral to another statutory agency. It was highly unlikely that a family was offered social work support. This raises questions about the likelihood of social workers understanding the impact on parents and children of poverty and environmental deprivation. It is to be hoped that the introduction of a new assessment framework will remedy this rather rigid approach, and it may change the narrowness of agency policies in respect of poverty (see DoH 2000b).

Table 7.1 *Number of services offered, according to category of need*

Category of need	One services	Two services	Three services	All cases per category
Intrinsic	2	3	3	13
Parental ill health	4	4	4	13
Family stress	10	12	6	36
Offending behaviour	–	2	1	6
Social deprivation	10	2	1	25
Total	**26**	**23**	**15**	**93**

Provision of long- or short-term services

The study looked at the duration of service provision along the dichotomy of *short-term services*, which were offered over a period of four weeks or less, and *longer-term* services lasting in excess of four weeks. The mean of service duration in this former group was two weeks and in the latter group 16 weeks. By far the largest number of families received short-term services (59) compared with 34 receiving longer-term services. The short-term services included cases where there had been a single interview. Sometimes this led to a referral elsewhere or to the case being closed. From the families' point of view, this short encounter was often seen as very valuable. Affording families the space to acknowledge and talk about their problems to a knowledgeable sympathetic listener should not be underestimated.

A number of factors can have an impact on the duration of service provision. These include:

- the category of need;

- the referral source;

- the gender of the children;

- the children's age group; and

- previous contact with Social Services.

The impact of the category of need. The children and families most likely to still be receiving services after eight weeks were those in the intrinsic need and offending behaviour categories. Children in need because of stress and parental ill health were just as likely to obtain a short- as a long-term service. This contrasted sharply with families in need through social deprivation, who were more likely to obtain services that lasted less than four weeks. The character of the services also varied according to the needs category. Those with intrinsic needs, parental illness and family stress were much more likely to receive multiple services. By contrast, in the needs category of social deprivation, families were much more likely to be given a single service. Nearly three-quarters of these families were offered a single service and less than a quarter were receiving multiple services.

The impact of the referral source. It was noticeable that just over half of the families who were professionally referred were still receiving services at the end of the study. Conversely, short-term services were more frequent among those who had referred themselves. In other words, the source of the referral was likely to influence the length of service. It is impossible to tell exactly why this is, but from talking to the families and the social workers it seems likely that, as suggested earlier, professional referrals were triggered when there were serious concerns and so they may well have merited a longer and more intensive service response. The threshold for the families' toleration of their problems was variable. Some turned to Social Services at an early stage whereas others spent some time attempting to solve the problems within their own resources and networks before seeking professional help.

The impact of the children's gender. There were fewer girls than boys participating in the study. The boys' cases were more likely to remain active for a longer period than those of the girls. In terms of short-term services, the boys and girls fared similarly. However, just over one-quarter of the girls were still receiving services at the end of the study compared with nearly half of the boys.

The impact of the children's ages. Generally, the younger the child, the greater was the likelihood of the case remaining active beyond the end of the study. The cases of the older children (over 12 years) were closed more quickly.

The impact of previous contact with Social Services. Previous contact of families with Social Services was associated with a longer period of service provision. In addition, there was a further association between the number of times families had been in contact with social services departments in the past and the length of services offered. We gained the impression that families had previously been helped with short-term support until problems became more serious. There are two ways of making sense of this. On the one hand, it may be that families need and benefit from the ongoing availability of relatively short-term and low-level support. Such a pattern can be seen to represent a responsive and sensitive approach by Social Services. On the other hand, it could be argued that the fact that some families continue to seek help over a sustained period could indicate that more substantial problems have not been identified and responded to. Parents interviewed in this study confirmed their appreciation of the availability of a service that they could access when they felt it was necessary. It is important that assessment procedures avoid the pitfall of only offering either a *substantial* service or *no* service. The challenge for professionals is to have a flexible response, guided by their own professional judgement but taking account of the preferences of the families.

The relationship between individual needs categories and service provision

We now move on to look at the provision of social services for children in need with an emphasis on the relationship between the categories of need and the services provided. Case studies are used to illustrate the complex and individual nature of the children's needs.

Children in intrinsic need

> **Definition:** Need relating to the children's own physical condition, developmental delay or difficulties; to physical illness or mental illness; to behaviour problems at home and/or at school.

This category includes self-harm, substance abuse, truanting/exclusion, bullying and unmanageable behaviour at home and at school. Disabled children were not within the scope of the project. To re-cap:

- there were 13 children in intrinsic need: nine boys and four girls;

- nine children in intrinsic need were professionally referred;

- children in intrinsic need represented just under one-quarter of all professional referrals;

- five children in intrinsic need were refused services;

- the children in intrinsic need who were refused services represented 17% of the children who were refused services;

- six of the children in intrinsic need who received services had more than one service; and

- one case of intrinsic need was short-term; and seven were long-term.

Individual problems

Within the category of intrinsic need, there was a range of problems:

- behavioural;

- health;

- social; and

- educational.

Intrinsic needs, although evident and distinct, could be associated with other family problems such as social deprivation and parents' mental health problems. For example, one child's severe behavioural problems put the parental relationship under particular stress.

Service provision served a dual purpose in addressing not only the children's needs but also the families' needs. Two case studies serve to illustrate the category of intrinsic need where services were provided:

● ●

A 15-year-old boy was suffering from drug-induced psychosis. He had been excluded from school for setting fire to a girl's hair; had run away from home and later had been found sleeping rough by the police. At the beginning of the study he was depressed. He had been treated in an adult psychiatric hospital, which was not considered by his parents to be meeting to his needs. The boy was clearly in need of help, but it was his parents who wanted to find services that they were satisfied would address his needs. By the end of the study the family had been allocated a social worker who had liaised with health services in order to find and fund a suitable, adolescent, therapeutic placement for the boy.

● ● ●

This hearing-impaired child was suffering from school phobia, which seemed to have been induced by bullying. Consequently, she did not want to go to school and often used to be taken there only for her to disappear again. This situation was compounded by other problems in the family. The house was dirty and in a state of disrepair. The mother had arthritis and was suffering from mobility problems. The elder sister often took the child to school, and the child's reluctance to go to school made them both late. A social worker was allocated, not only to address the child's non-attendance at school but also to support the work with the family in improving their domestic circumstances, including cleaning and repairs.

● ●

Children in need through parental ill health

Definition: Need because of parental illness, mental and physical; addiction, depression or severe stress.

To re-cap:

♦ there were 13 children in need through parental ill health: eight boys and five girls;

♦ ten of the children in need through parental ill health were professionally referred;

♦ children in need through parental ill health represented one-quarter of professional referrals;

♦ one child in need through parental ill health was refused services;

♦ all the children in need through parental ill health who did receive services received in excess of two; and

♦ six cases of need through parental ill health were short-term; and six were long-term.

Children in need through parental illness were a high priority for Social Services. The only family in this category who did not obtain a service involved a case of maternal depression. Although the mother was referred by the health visitor, Social Services assessed that her need was not so severe as to place her children at risk of impairment or, as she herself commented cynically, 'they had not got it as badly as some'.

The need for help in caring for the children arose in various ways:

- emergency admission to hospital;

- planned admission to hospital in the course of illness;

- depression, particularly post-natal depression; and

- parents' learning difficulties.

A case study serves to illustrate the children's needs in a situation where the mother was admitted to hospital:

Two children, aged 10 and 11, needed help when their mother, who suffered from multiple sclerosis, was admitted to hospital from time to time. A home help was provided and respite care was made available, which could be longer term. Long-term planning was evident in this case: in order to plan for the mother's gradual deterioration and eventual death, a care plan was made with the aim of providing permanent placement for the children.

Children in need through family stress

Definition: Need as a result of living within an unstable, conflictual, and emotionally or developmentally damaging family.

To re-cap:

- there were 36 children in the study who were in need through family stress: 25 boys and 11 girls;

- 14 children in need through family stress were professionally referred;

- children in need through family stress represented 35% of professional referrals;

- eight children in need through family stress were refused services;

- children in need through family stress represented just over one-quarter of the children who were refused services;

- 18 of the 28 children in need through family stress who received services received packages of care, 12 having two and six having three services; and

- 14 cases of need through family stress were short-term; 15 were long-term.

Children in need through family stress were frequently in situations of conflict, both indirectly, between parents and ex-partners, and directly, between stepparents and stepchildren.

The children who received services were often showing immediate, if sometimes short-lived, distress. For example, an 8-year-old child caught up in a custody dispute between her parents started self-harming. Services made a substantial difference. Another 8-year-old girl wanted support in the context of parental arguments about contact that she did not want. Social work support with the whole family helped to resolve the differences and meant that the girl's wishes were taken into account.

Children in need through offending behaviour

Definition: Need because of offending behaviour, breaking the law.

The low numbers in this category reflect the fact that the majority of children who commit crimes are dealt with within specialist juvenile justice teams and not in generic social work children and family teams. To re-cap:

- there were six children in need through offending behaviour, all boys;

- one child in need through offending behaviour was professionally referred;

- three children in need through offending behaviour were refused services;

- the three children who received services had packages of care, two having two and one having three services; and

- three cases of need through offending behaviour were long-term.

Only three children in this category were offered a service. In addition to their offending behaviour, these children all had severe behavioural problems and mental health problems. Two were from families with problems of substance abuse, as the following case studies show:

● ●

A boy of 14 who had a medical condition of Attention-Deficit Hyperactivity Disorder, was violent towards his sister within the home and towards other children outside. He had a history of stealing. His parents requested respite care for him and help in 'giving him a fright'. Social Services provided respite care for the child in conjunction with counselling for the parents.

● ● ●

A 13-year-old boy, whose mother approached Social Services because of his shoplifting, truanting and vandalism, was assessed by the social worker and subsequently provided with a multi-agency service including psycho-therapy, a place in a youth group and extra tutoring at school.

● ●

Children in need through social deprivation

Definition: Need because of deprivation, poverty or social disadvantage.

To re-cap:

- ◆ there were 25 children in need through social deprivation: 11 boys and 14 girls;

- ◆ five children in need through social deprivation were professionally referred;

- ◆ children in need through social deprivation represented just under one-seventh of professional referrals;

- ◆ 12 children in need through social deprivation were refused services;

- ◆ children in need through social deprivation represented two-fifths of the children who were refused services;

- ◆ three of the 13 children who received services had packages of care, two having two and one having three services; and

- ◆ nine cases of need through social deprivation were short-term, four were long-term.

Social deprivation needs were of two types: general problems and specific problems. The following case study illustates a case of racial abuse which also involved other problems.

• •

Three children – two boys aged 12 and 15, and a girl aged 8 years – lived with their single-parent mother. The children were of dual parentage. This family's needs were multiple. The whole family had been the subject of verbal and physical abuse which seemed to be racially motivated. The fabric of the house was very poor, including a serious damp problem. One child had asthma and another was just recovering from pneumonia. The family needed help in arranging a housing transfer. In addition, the mother had serious health problems including diabetes, which necessitated a special diet. Income was restricted to the mother's invalidity benefit; there was no income support because the father was perceived by DSS to still be part of the family even though he was not.

• •

The range and type of services that the families received

This section examines in greater depth the range of (Children Act 1989) Part III services that were offered to children in need and to their families. The services provided had two main components, which were sometimes provided together, sometimes separately:

♦ social work, which appears in the Children Act 1989 as 'advice, guidance and counselling'; and

♦ other services, named specifically in Volume 2 of *Guidance and Regulations* (DoH 1991) and include day care services, befriending services, parent/toddler groups, toy libraries, drop-in centres, play buses, family centres, accommodation, reunification arranged by the social worker or others.

In order to capture the range and creativity of social services activity we have provided a group of case studies, some of which illustrate the provision of social work support on its own, while others illustrate the incorporation of such support within the specific services we discovered had been provided.

Social work

A total of 22 cases were allocated to a social worker and offered short- or long-term, direct or indirect support. Families of children in need aged over 12 years were less likely to receive social work: just under two-fifths, compared with half of the children under 12 years of age. As noted above, it was part of a general trend for families of older children to be refused services (52% overall).

Social work was offered to families with a wide range of needs, often, but not exclusively, to families whose needs arose from or were centred on a particular child rather than to families where the needs of a child arose from family circumstances. Case studies serve to illustrate social work support in each type of situation:

● ●

A 6-year-old girl was displaying extreme behaviour problems; she 'won't do nowt, wrecked her bedroom, last year she set fire to her bed'. The family had an allocated social worker who undertook a focused piece of direct work with the child, concentrating on building her self-esteem and helping the child to understand the dynamics of the family.

● ● ●

An 8-year-old boy whose parents had split up had regular contact visits with his father as part of an informal arrangement. On one occasion, however, the father wanted to keep the child and promised him toys to bribe him to stay. The father and paternal grandmother, who lived in the same house, did not let the child's mother speak to him on the telephone. In the end, his mother resorted to snatching him back. Her son was extremely distressed and started self-harming, scratching his face and having tantrums. His mother was worried about the damage that this would cause and approached Social Services. She had an appointment within a week, and the social worker talked to her and reassured her that her child's behaviour was not inappropriate in the context of the anxiety the child must have been through. The worker undertook a short piece of task-centred work with the mother, reinforcing her capabilities and helping her to sort out the legalities of contact arrangements. The mother's commented:

> I just feel that on the whole they saw me very quickly, which in view of what was happening was imperative. I couldn't have waited a week or two weeks. He was absolutely on the ball . . . apart from the fairly obvious bits like saying what a brilliant mother I was and how well I was doing, he also said I should

see a solicitor just to get the legal things. And at the time that was the last thing on my mind. And he just sort of focused everything.

• •

When a whole family needed support and there were multiple problems, social workers undertook both direct work and work that facilitated liaison with others. Social workers would work in a variety of ways with families:

♦ providing emotional support for the family;

♦ liaising with health and education services;

♦ identifying other services that could help; and

♦ developing parenting skills.

Two case studies serve to illustrate that a complexity of needs requires social work as the lynchpin of a range of other services. These cases also demonstrate the overlap between the different needs categories. Even though the first referral was because of the mother's health problems, there were many other stresses on the family.

• •

A 21-year-old mother of three children under 4 years of age had recently had a new baby and split up from her husband in violent and acrimonious circumstances, with police involvement. She was on medication for post-natal depression and was in regular contact with the primary health-care team. She felt she could not cope on her own and asked her health visitor to get in touch with Social Services. The family lived in an isolated rural area. Two children suffered from asthma, and one of the children had a cleft palate. The social worker constructed a family support plan that included social work support in collaboration with the health visitor, a play group for the children, and a family support worker for a couple of hours a week to support her and to carry out tasks around the house.

• • •

An 8-year-old juvenile offender, whose parents had a number of problems of their own, including alcoholism, not only obtained a social worker who worked closely with the family but also had a sessional worker as an outreach service. His father said:

[The social worker] talks about how things are with the children and that . . . and gives us ideas about how to deal with them . . . she helps us to discipline them . . . This social worker is OK. She's arranging for him to go down to the police station and play pool with them, so that he knows, like, that not all policemen are bad, because he doesn't have a very good relationship with them. The sessional worker takes him out and does things with him. He took him boxing last week to try and get rid of some of his aggression.

Other Part III services

The range of services

It was heartening to find that a wide range of Part III services were offered. These included:

- family support workers to befriend families;

- short-term accommodation;

- under-fives' day care;

- club and sporting activities;

- family centres; and

- support groups.

Although families may have asked for a particular service about which they had heard or that they had used on a previous occasion, they were sometimes offered an equally or more effective alternative. Social workers clearly used their judgement to link families to existing resources. For example, parents of children who had behavioural problems might have requested short-term accommodation, but when they were offered such accommodation, social workers worked with the children on behaviour problems during the placement.

Family support workers

As a previous case study illustrates, families who were experiencing parental illness often had a mixture of both chronic and acute physical and mental health problems that made it difficult for them to look after their children and carry out household tasks. For example, the mother of a newly born baby had both post-natal depression and a chronic back problem. Family support workers provided both emotional support and practical help, and their input was often combined with a range of other services. One parent explained:

I get a support worker. And she's found me a child-minder who will start next week, for six hours a week. Someone comes in to me two hours a week and the personal care person comes in twice a week. And she's also contacted Homestart . . . She normally does practical things . . . feeding, changing, hoovering, dusting, whatever I ask her to do. They offer help and support for the family, bits and pieces, whatever I ask.

Short-term accommodation

Seven families asked for short-term accommodation (respite care) for their children. In fact, 13 families were provided with this service. Short-term accommodation was seen by families as a positive family support service, which met both the needs of the children and their parents.

Although the majority of short-term accommodation was offered to children in need through family stress (seven cases), the service was also provided for children in other categories of need: parental ill health, intrinsic need and offending behaviour.

Day care

Twelve parents asked for day care. The majority were living in conditions of social deprivation and had health problems, such as post-natal depression, and family problems that resulted in stress. Eleven of the 12 families were offered day care, and the majority had children in need through family stress and parental illness One family was offered day care for a younger child of the family although the designated 'child in need' was an older child.

Club and sporting activities and holidays

A combination of after-school and holiday activities – sports, dancing, hobbies and holidays – were offered to 12 children in need, to occupy them during their spare time or in the long summer holidays, which is always a particularly difficult time for mothers. This service covered several needs categories: family stress, parental health problems, social deprivation and offending behaviour.

Generally the service was offered to ameliorate problems relating to the children's behaviour. Some behavioural problems were extreme, including violence and aggression or intimidation of younger siblings. Others resulted from the parents feeling unable to manage their children's behaviour, a feeling that could have been exacerbated by parental ill health. In one family, the mother suffered from multiple sclerosis and was conscious that her 8-year-old son was restricted because of her condition. She wanted her son to go to an after-school club that was attended by many of his friends.

These services had several purposes:

- to give the parents a break from their children;
- to give the children a break from their parents;
- to allow the children to use excess energy; and
- to give the children an opportunity to build up some sense of self-worth by pursuing an interest.

Direct work with children

Direct work with children, offered to seven families, had a number of purposes:

- the changing of specific behaviours;
- reflective case work, for example to help children cope with loss and bereavement; and
- building social skills and raising self-esteem by participation in activities such as swimming, outings with the worker.

The children who were offered direct work, all aged over 6 years, were displaying a range of behavioural problems. Some were behaving aggressively, others were withdrawn and somewhat depressed. For example, a 14-year-old girl had reacted badly both to her mother's new partner and to a move from one region to another. The mother was finding her behaviour difficult to manage and asked for her to be accommodated. Instead, the direct work was offered through a short-term programme of planned sessions. The worker helped the girl to tackle her behaviour, involved her in various activities, and took her swimming and then out for a meal to build up her social skills.

Family centres

Family centre support was generally given to families of younger children, under the age of 12. Six families obtained this support, within the needs categories of family stress, offending behaviour and parental illness. The children had individual behavioural problems in the context of the problems experienced by the families as a whole. The use of a family centre by the parents enabled them to meet others in like circumstances and develop and enhance their parenting skills. At the same time, the staff in the centre were able to offer extra attention and support to the children in their own right. A case study serves to illustrate the reasons for making a family centre available:

A 6-year-old had unmanageable behaviour and also suffered food allergies. Her mother suffered from arthritis and was wheelchair-bound. Both parents were less than confident in their parenting and found it difficult to challenge their daughter's behaviour, which had deteriorated. An assessment of the family was made at the local family centre where the parents were helped to set boundaries for their daughter and to be more assertive. In addition, the family were offered resources for the daughter to have dancing lessons, so that she could do something that she would enjoy and which would give her self-confidence.

Support group

Two families in which the parents were in their 20s were offered membership of a support group, which was designed as a network for young parents in the area. For example, two children aged 5 and 7, had a mother with chronic physical health problems. She had some support from her mother but otherwise was rather isolated. The children were offered a number of activities, and the parent was invited to a local support group where she could meet other young parents and carers and be involved in a range of activities.

Other services

Just over half of the parents in the study looked to Social Services to obtain for them other services such as financial assistance or help with accessing housing, education or health services. In fact, just over a third obtained the services they were seeking. The provision of these services was most likely to be given to parents who specifically requested them. Families who had a less specific idea of what would help them were less likely to be referred elsewhere, even though they had multiple problems.

Over half of the families with children in need because of parental ill health were offered other services, in particular help with accessing health services or community care. By contrast, well under a quarter of the families with children in need through social deprivation received other services, such as help with housing or financial assistance. Families with children in intrinsic need or in need through family stress were also less likely to obtain other services. Only one of the six families with children in need because of offending behaviour obtained other services.

It is of note that 'other services provision' was highest for children who were aged under 12 years. This suggests that there continues to be an emphasis by Social Services on providing resources to safeguard younger children, and that the presence of older children is less likely to be acknowledged as coming within the remit of Social Services unless the children are looked after by them.

Help with health-related services

Seventeen families wanted help in dealing with health-related services for themselves or for their children. Their circumstances included both parental physical and mental health needs and children's behavioural problems.

Twelve families obtained this help across several needs categories, including offending behaviour. It was of note that health-related needs were widespread across the different needs categories and appeared to have a powerful negative impact on family dynamics.

Only four parents were referred to health services in their own right. These parents either had mental health problems, such as problem drinking and depression, or chronic or acute physical health problems. It appears that social workers were most anxious to acknowledge and refer mental health problems because they understood the impact of these on the children. They tended to give a lower priority to parental physical health needs, even when the impact of these on parenting ability was noticeable. This underlines the importance of recognising the Children Act principle that parents have needs in their own right, and that only by addressing these needs will the welfare of the child be promoted.

By contrast, where health problems were identified on the part of the children, social workers acted very quickly and obtained a wide range of services, including referrals to counsellors, psychologists, child psychiatrists, child and family therapists and multidisciplinary child and family consultation centres.

A 6-year-old girl lived with her father, stepmother and new twin siblings. Her birth mother had emigrated to the United States. The child had developed behavioural problems in response to the new family situation. The father, who was away from home on an oil rig, told Social Services:

She tells lies; we do not know what to believe. She 'cries wolf'. She lies her way out of things. She should have been an only child. As long as she is the centre of attention, she is no trouble.

Her stepmother broke her wrist in a car accident and was unable to carry out basic household tasks. There were thus several interlinked problems in the family. To address the relationship difficulties between the child and the family Social Services negotiated a counsellor from child and family therapy services. In addition, a home help was arranged to assist the parents with household tasks.

Help with education services

Nine families whose children were truanting or had been excluded from school wanted help with education services. These parents wanted professional support in dealing with education departments, whom they had earlier found unresponsive when they approached them directly. All the families were very concerned that their children be helped back into mainstream education and felt that their children's educational development and attainment was being put at risk by the delays on the part of the education department. In fact, only four families obtained this help. Social Services liaised with the education authority in order to organise services.

A 10-year-old child had very severe behavioural problems both at home and at school: he was violent and difficult to control at school and had learning difficulties and poor concentration. The school had reached the limits of their abilities to contain his behaviour and had suggested that a special school place might be appropriate. However, the placement needed joint funding. The mother had been wanting special care for her son for a long time and had found a school she felt met her son's needs. In fact, the problems with the child were not purely educational, so planning meetings were held between professionals from the departments of health, education and social services in order to determine the best source of care for the child and who would fund it.

In the end, the child was not sent to the school of the mother's choice, and of the professionals' preference, because of funding constraints. The matter was left unresolved, with the child being in danger of exclusion from the original school. The mother was left frustrated and angry feeling let down by both social services and education departments.

● ●

This case underlines the significance of funding arrangements; if these are not appropriate they can subvert the intention of the social services staff to operate on a need-led basis.

Help with housing

Parents sought a variety of help from Social Services to remedy their housing problems. These included:

♦ support for housing applications;

♦ support for transfer applications;

♦ intervention in cases of rent arrears; and

♦ refugee settlement.

Fourteen families wanted help with housing. All were facing conditions of severe social deprivation, although family stress, intrinsic need and parental ill health were also identified as being associated with the housing problems. Inappropriate, overcrowded living conditions were the main problems that led families to request help with housing.

Only four of the 14 families obtained help with housing. Social workers had a clear role as advocates in all these cases. In two cases, which were unsuccessful, they aimed to obtain a housing transfer by writing letters to the council. Both families were in the same geographical area, one where the council had a particularly stringent points system for allocating properties. The third family needed central heating, and the social worker talked to the council about installation. The advocacy of Social Services was successful in the case of the fourth family. All the families manifested high levels of family stress, social deprivation and intrinsic need.

A case study serves to illustrate the housing assistance given by Social Services:

• •

A mother with two young children aged 1 and 3 had approached Social
Services because of her son's health problems: he had childhood convulsions.
He shared a room with his sister and could easily have fits while she was there,
which was potentially distressing. Her husband had emphysema and was finding
it increasingly difficult to move around. He would eventually be wheelchair-
bound and was already finding it difficult to climb stairs. In addition, the house
in which they lived was damp. Social Services assessed the situation for the
family and applied on their behalf for a housing transfer, which was successful.

• •

Financial help

Sixteen families wanted financial help in the form of Section 17 payments.
Fifteen of these families had children in need through social deprivation. The
level of their poverty was evident from the extent to which they had felt it
necessary to approach Social Services for everyday items such as food, clothing, electricity and nappies; for housing items such as cots, carpets, beds,
refrigerators and cookers; and for special expenditure such as school uniform.
Many of these families were already heavily in debt.

Nine families obtained Section 17 funding; six of them had children in the
needs category of social deprivation. In spite of this high level of poverty, when
they approached Social Services the parents were containing their own stress
and endeavouring to parent their children and keep their household going.

Social Services were asked to provide financial help for 11 families, either
directly by the families themselves or by health personnel. These families
wanted financial help for the following reasons: household items; rent;
deposit so that a family subjected to racial abuse could leave the area; baby
equipment; school uniform; carpets for a new home. A case study serves to
illustrate both Section 17 payments and recourse to charitable funding:

• •

Four children lived in a small three-bedroom maisonette on which there were
rent arrears. The father described his situation:
> It all revolved round money . . . I couldn't afford school uniform for my son
> . . . and then at the same time the council were after me for rent arrears . . .
> I know it was my fault really, but they never sent me a reminder to renew my

housing benefit, and then I owed them an awful lot of rent. I was surprised and really pleased. We were facing eviction, and they wrote off to the Charities Board (for the rent arrears) and they paid off all the debt. And [Social Services] helped us with school uniform. We weren't expecting that.

● ●

Community care

Five parents, all with children under school age, wanted short-term help with household tasks. The parents were incapacitated either through serious health problems, including post-natal depression, or because of accidents. Two families obtained short-term help with household tasks from community care teams.

● ●

A 14-year-old boy had behavioural problems and was falling behind at school, where he had been kept down to repeat a year. A substantial part of his educational problems stemmed from his role as a young carer to his mother, who had a hearing impairment and serious mobility problems resulting from childhood polio. Social Services referred the mother to the adult social work team, who put her on touch with a local society for hearing impaired people. In addition, direct social work was provided for the youngster, who was also invited to attend a specialist youth group for children who were young carers.

● ●

Summary

Two-fifths of the the families knew within one week whether they would be allocated services. Just under three-quarters knew within two weeks. The quickest response was when no service was to be provided.

Two-fifths of the families who had referred themselves were not offered services, compared to just under a fifth of families referred by professionals.

Professionally referred families received *more* services over *longer* periods.

Service provision varied according to category of need. Cases of social deprivation were least likely to be offered services. By contrast, cases of parental ill health were most likely to be offered services; cases of family stress to a lesser extent.

Cases that involved boys, younger children and families with a longer previous history of contact with Social Services remained active longer than others.

There was a clear link between the type of services requested and the service obtained in cases of parental ill health, offending behaviour and social deprivation. There was no such link between cases of family stress and intrinsic need and the subsequent service.

A wider range of services was offered than was requested. Short-term accommodation, day care and activities were frequently offered as an alternative to the request for long-term accommodation.

8

The families' verdict on Social Services

This chapter focuses on the views of families in response to the provision of social services for their children in need, including their view of service deficits. In other words, we explore the views of families as to the way in which their circumstances *did* improve, as well as their view of the effect of *not* getting services or *not* getting the anticipated benefit from the service they *were* offered.

The parents' views: responses and outcomes

We asked the parents what they expected from the service. At the end of the period of service the parents were revisited to explore perceived/gains and unfulfilled expectations. The four dimensions that the parents had identified with the researchers at the beginning of the study as important to them were:

- ◆ relief of stress;
- ◆ help with child development;
- ◆ improvement in family relationships; and
- ◆ alleviation of practical problems.

Table 8.1 indicates the connection between the parents' anticipation of the perceived benefits and how far those expectations were fulfilled.

Table 8.1 *Anticipated and confirmed benefits: the parents' view*

Benefits*	Parents anticipating benefit	Parents obtaining benefit	
	No.	No.	%
Relief of stress	66	48	73
Help with child development	40	31	78
Improvement in family relationships	39	16	41
Alleviation of practical problems	28	28	100

* Categories are not mutually exclusive

Many families, across the range of needs categories, appreciated the help provided by Social Services and felt that their expectations had been fulfilled. In some cases, parents were disappointed that the services did not make the difference they had anticipated. Some might have been over-optimistic or had unrealistic expectations of the power and resources of Social Services. In other cases, there were questions about the length and nature of the service. Nevertheless, they were often appreciative of the manner in which social workers had conducted their business.

Relief of stress

Whether parents approached Social Services for short- or long-term help, relief from stress in some form was a high priority in terms of anticipated benefits in 66 cases. Families who were experiencing problems with their children's behaviour felt that they needed someone to talk to for support and advice, especially if they were scared about harming their children, and in order to relieve their stress through joint problem-solving. Other parents were at the end of their tether and highly stressed by unproductive encounters with other professionals.

Seventy-three per cent of the 66 parents who had hoped the services would reduce their levels of stress had their expectations met. Relief from stress took the following forms:

- personal support;

- family support;

- avoidance of an escalation of problems into a child protection issue;

- problem-solving and taking control; and

- just listening.

Case studies serve to illustrate the range of support that was appreciated. The first case study shows that relief of stress could be experienced regardless of the outcome of approaching Social Services in terms of looking for a cure for the problems:

• •

A mother had initially approached Social Services because her 3-year-old child had intrinsic needs in the form of an epileptic condition that caused convulsions. In fact, there were many family problems: the mother suffered from depression and was subject to violence from her husband, who had a degenerative disease and was becoming progressively wheelchair-bound. The family lived in overcrowded accommodation. Although Social Services supported the family in a housing transfer to a larger house in a different area, the mother remained depressed and the marital relationship deteriorated further. However, the mother commented:

> When I met [the social worker] my whole outlook on Social Services changed. They were there for me. They have been there every time for me. I had a real barrier about them . . . they've done good for me every time. I've never had to moan or anything. When I moved I sent her a thank-you letter, just for all her help and backup and just for being there really. Today, she's not even my social worker, I 'phoned her up and she was there to listen . . . she's an absolute diamond.

The second case study shows that emotional support was not restricted to social work support:

> A single mother, who was having difficulty coping with three young boys aged 5–9, had obtained support from a family centre. She commented:
>> It's made me a lot stronger and able to cope better. I don't always give in to them now. If it wasn't for them, I don't know what they would be like now or anything.

The third case study demonstrates the efficacy of social work support in the prevention of a situation escalating into one of serious abuse:

> A young single mother, recently separated from her husband, was suffering from depression. She was caring for three children under 7, the youngest of whom was new-born. Initially the mother was wary of approaching Social Services. She was particularly concerned because she was hitting the eldest of her children and feared the consequences. She said of the help she received through social work support:
>> It has been much appreciated . . . I was able to talk to the social worker about hitting him . . . I could have lost control if I did not get help. At the time I just got flack from my friends, because they said I didn't care for my children . . . I know I've got someone to turn to.

The following comments demonstrate the value of social work support that is carried out in partnership with parents and thus enables them to take control of their problem situations:

● ●

It helped me to calm down, to look at things objectively, and to take positive action to help him. I don't think there is anything else they can do for me now.

● ●

One parent outlined the value of talking to a professional who is perceived as open-minded and objective:

● ●

They listened to what you've got to say. Like when I first told my sister, she didn't listen to me, she just shouted and bawled, whereas they actually sat and listened to me, to what I'd got to say.

● ●

Twenty-seven per cent of the families felt Social Services responded inappropriately to their stress, as the following case studies demonstrate:

● ●

An older mother, whose husband had just left her for a younger woman, approached Social Services for both personal support and financial help. She lived in a pleasant residential area and was an owner-occupier. One of her children had attended a private kindergarten. She was refused services on the grounds that she could seek help within the private sector. The mother felt she had been turned away because of her seeming prosperity. In fact, she had been left with considerable family debts. She had turned to social workers because she believed they could offer a confidential and professional service.

● ● ●

A young Pakistani mother with four children under the age of 6 was experiencing domestic violence and had no extended family other than her husband's. English was not her first language, and the problems caused in the initial interview by the absence of interpreting facilities meant that she was deterred from returning to see the social worker who was allocated five weeks later. Through an interpreter she said:

I was very nervous and aware that my community would not approve of my betraying family confidences. I had gone because my friend told me she had been helped by social workers. It left me feeling I had to cope on my own and hope everything will turn out all right.

I was so stressed. I just needed someone to understand and help me. I think because I didn't look down-and-out, I was turned away. I wish I had worn some old clothes from Oxfam. I left feeling even more desperate.

Help with child development

Almost half of the parents in the study anticipated that contact with Social Services would help their children's development. Seventy-eight per cent of these parents felt that the social provision of social services had helped them in this way. There were several areas of intervention.

Direct services for children

Parents appreciated the stimulation provided by playgroups and child-minders. In many cases Social Services also addressed the children's behavioural problems. Comments from case studies serve to illustrate, first, how unmanageable behaviour could be changed and, second, how children could be helped to develop social skills and self-confidence:

The children are behaving a little more. They have their days when they're driving me mad . . . I seem to have a bit more control over him. He is calmer and listening to a few people now. He runs away less, and he's taking things in.
I think it's a case now that he has to. A lot of people have been moaning at him, you know; he's told from the family centre and all that: 'You just can't do that'. And I think he might be slightly taking it all in now . . . I think he's starting to realise that he can't get away with everything any more. I think he thought he could just go [to the family centre] for an hour a week and just do what he liked, but it's not like that. He got the hump last week because he wanted to play on the computer all the time and he wasn't allowed.

'She's calmed down a lot and she's a lot happier in herself ... Before she went to nursery she was quite clingy and when she went there, for a while she was crying ... It's made a difference, like when she first went to playschool she just went in, she was quite happy.'

Time apart was a benefit to both parents. Children could be restricted socially because of social deprivation, isolation or the parents' disabilities. For example, through direct work with children, Social Services took children on outings as an opportunity for a break from home and to deal with behavioural problems. As one parent commented:

> The social worker has been helpful with transport and taken him out on outings and talked to him. She has been a great support. Better behaviour from him. He's now quite helpful in the home.

The opportunity created for children to talk was appreciated:

> He got a lot of things off his chest about his father. It was good for him to talk to someone neutral . . . It helped him more than us. He knows that there is somebody that he can talk to. If he was in that situation once again, he could go back and talk to them. We shouldn't be so floored by it all. He doesn't have to bottle it up. It's someone to listen to him and not just tell him off, I think. We didn't realise that the situation with the father had got to him so much. He opened our eyes a bit . . . The father didn't want a boy for a start, that was half the problem.

Activities for children also offered them the opportunity to mix socially, with positive results:

> [It] increased his self-esteem, [to] find something that he can do, give him a chance in life ... everyone needs something that they can do.

At the same time, family centres helped both carers and children to benefit from time apart by giving carers space and allowing children to mix. A mother commented:

> She is so forward for her age, with numbers and colours and everything. She has really come out of herself. A little whiz-kid. We all get on a lot better for it too.'

The planned activities also used children's energy more productively:

> It helped me and it helped him because he needs to run round and burn off energy.

Unmet expectations

Parents whose expectations were not met felt social workers did not appreciate the difficulties a child presented to the family. There was often a mismatch between official assessment of need and need as perceived by the parents. These families included a couple with a child with learning disabilities. Their frustration arose from the fact that they expected the social worker to help them obtain a place for their child in a special school. As the social worker felt there was no evidence that the child's current school was inappropriate, no action was taken. This left the parents feeling angry. The father said:

> We knew another family where social workers got their child transferred.
> We were angry they put us off and didn't seem to believe us.

Improvement in family relationships

Improvement in family relationships could take two forms: between children in need and their families or between partners. Just over two-fifths of the families in the study were hoping that the intervention of Social Services would improve family relationships; 41% of these families confirmed that this had been achieved. In particular, carers who were having difficulty with their children's behaviour were concerned about the negative impact not only on the well-being of other children in the family but also on the parental partnership. The comment from one mother serves to illustrate the benefits to family relationships:

⦿ ⦿

> It gave me a break and it gave me time to get my thoughts together . . .
> It gave me and my husband a little time on our own . . . I was in a desperate
> state. When you are in that depressed situation you feel that there has got to
> be someone out there who can help.

⦿ ⦿

The experience of one mother shows how Social Services can provide an opportunity for a parent to learn coping techniques to develop confidence for dealing with future problem situations:

> Everything is a lot better than it was last time. My relationship with my
> husband and child and my health. I feel much stronger and would cope better
> if it happened again.

The overlap of benefits (noted in Chapter 7) is evident in the following comments; which clearly describe both relief of stress and an improvement in family relationships:

> It helped to talk about the case and we can always talk again . . . We're not
> so stressed out as before . . . someone is listening to us . . . things really

calmed down. My husband and I were taking it out on each other until we saw the social worker.

Unmet expectations

Most of the unmet expectations related to the fact that parents, usually mothers, hoped Social Services would 'sort out' their partner. Social Services generally felt this was beyond their remit unless there was evidence that the child's welfare was being affected, as the following case study shows:

● ●

A mother of two teenage children, who had received many family services in the past, approached Social Services about her partner's drinking problems. She said:

They couldn't get round to the house quick enough when the kids were little. Now I'm asking for help for me, they don't want to know.

● ●

Alleviation of practical problems or specific needs

Almost a third of families in the study hoped that Social Services would provide immediate practical help, either as the only service required or in conjunction with other, ongoing, services. All the parents who hoped to obtain practical services did in fact receive them.

The parents appreciated rapid intervention on a practical level in times of crisis. Comments from case studies serve to illustrate the range of specific, practical needs:

● ●

I was surprised and really pleased. We were facing eviction, and they wrote off to the Charities Board for the rent arrears and they paid off all the debt. And they helped us with school uniform. We weren't expecting that.

● ● ●

Our cooker was condemned, and I was already up to the limit on my Social Fund loan . . . so they agreed to lend us the money for a second-hand cooker.

● ● ●

Well, we've just moved, and I didn't have any spare cash to buy any carpets
. . . so I went to the Social Services and they applied to the Charities Board for
me . . . and they gave us the money for the carpets . . . now the girls can run
around and I don't need to worry.'

● ● ●

Well, they got in touch with the council and got us help with the heating . . .
It's been a problem for a long while . . . I was worried about the winter
months.

● ●

Benefits according to category of need

Expectations and outcomes showed some differences across the needs categories. For example, parents presenting ill health problems had their
expectations exceeded in every case. By comparison, in social deprivation
cases, expectations exceeded provision in all cases. In between came the category of family stress: parents mostly obtained benefits in terms of reduction
of stress, but were less satisfied in terms of seeing their family relationships
improve. In cases of offending behaviour, half of the families achieved the
anticipated outcomes.

The children's views: positive responses and beneficial outcomes

The children we interviewed were hoping to achieve a number of benefits.
For example, just under two-fifths of children, all in the family stress
category, were hoping that parental conflict would be resolved. A smaller
number of children, all in the intrinsic needs group, wanted help with their
behaviour and a break from their families. Where social deprivation was an
issue, the children hoped for financial and practical support.

Children saw the provision of support activities as important outcomes for
themselves. A small number saw help with schooling or time away from
home as important. Support was an important outcome for children in need
through family stress. Children in need through social deprivation were not
aware of having obtained any services at all.

Almost half of the children were happy that Social Services were involved
in their families' problems, a third were not bothered and the rest were

unhappy about their families' involvement with Social Services. Of the children who were unhappy, a third had intrinsic needs, almost a quarter were in need through family stress and the rest were in need through social deprivation or parental ill health.

Almost half of the children were pleased with the services offered, just over a third were neither pleased nor displeased and the rest were displeased. Almost three-quarters of the children were happy with the outcome overall.

The parents' responses to different types of service provision

The majority (86%) of parents who approached or were referred to Social Services viewed the contact as sympathetic and helpful. Within needs categories there was some variation. Although parents of children with intrinsic needs received a higher proportion of the services requested than parents of children with other needs, they tended to be most dissatisfied. In contrast, almost all the parents of children in need because of parental illness found Social Services sympathetic and helpful.

Interpreting these findings needs to take account of the broad span of problems covered by the intrinsic need category. For example, a social worker with little specialist knowledge of medical problems such as epilepsy or Attention -Deficit Hyperactivity Disorder might have missed important aspects of the problems. By contrast, the health needs of parents were more likely to be referred to others who were more expert.

Satisfied families

The following case studies illustrate the range of services provided and the high level of satisfaction with the services:

● ●

A family approached Social Services with multiple problems: a 3-year-old child suffered from convulsions; the father was violent and disabled; the mother had general depression. Despite the ongoing nature of her problems, the mother was very pleased with the package of support that she obtained from Social Services and did not feel that there was any more that they could do for the family.

● ● ●

A mother of three children aged 5–9 years had previously had a great deal of contact with Social Services. At the beginning of the study, she was feeling depressed but did not really see that referral to a family centre could help. The family obtained multiple services from Social Services, including liaison with a number of agencies to help the eldest child, who was not only difficult to control at school but also at home. He frequently ran away and lied to his mother. At the end of the study, the mother felt that the services had helped and said that she 'felt more positive' about the situation and more in control of her life.

● ● ●

A mother of three children under the age of 7 had recently been left by her husband. She had been feeling depressed but at the end of the study expressed her satisfaction with the amount of help that she was having: she now felt supported. 'I've gone from feeling totally alone to getting help from everywhere.'

● ●

Families whose problems were not solved by Social Services

Among these families it is important to distinguish between parents who had different issues. Briefly these can be catalogued as:

- ◆ families dissatisfied with Social Services;

- ◆ families unsatisfied with the extent of services; and

- ◆ families whose needs had changed or who had found other sources of help.

● ●

It is important to distinguish between the notions of 'unsatisfied' and 'dissatisfied'. Many of the families were unsatisfied in that they would have liked a greater amount of service, but they were not dissatisfied with the quality of the service they had received.

Families dissatisfied with Social Services

The following quotes from case studies serve to illustrate parents' dissatisfaction with Social Services in terms of what they perceived as inadequate interventions. Dissatisfaction arose from communication problems and inappropriate expectations:

They don't listen to the real facts of the story: that you're broke; you're living on your nerves; that you have a child who absolutely has such a violent nature, you don't know which way to turn, and you want some help. You want to be told: 'I'll ring this person, I'll ring that person. Have you tried this, have you tried that?' . . . But they don't. They look at you and think: 'Why is she behaving like that, is this an abused child, is that what she is trying to say?'

The first time I went to Social Services I walked out bewildered. They didn't explain what they were there for. Was it talking, practical help? I didn't understand what they were saying.

I thought they were capable of a lot more than they have actually done. I got the impression that the children and families department were there to help families with a lot of problems, but they didn't, especially when they didn't get back to me over his clothing. I had to 'phone them and they didn't get back and I said: 'I'm not going to ring them.'

I assumed that Social Services were about this . . . I got a picture in my head about what they did, for others. But it is really not the same. So many other people had said they'd helped them get this, they helped them get that, they were really good . . . maybe I didn't go the right way around things. You don't know. I thought: 'Oh well, it was worth a try.' I thought I'd get a lot more help than I did.

I have to do all the leg work. I need someone to do the contacting. I am told to ring charities, but which charities? It is left to me to get money out of them. I don't know where to start. There should be an organisation which liaises with charities.

Families unsatisfied with the extent of the services

Unsatisfied families were those who spoke positively about the services they had been given but would have liked more, or wanted other services that were unavailable. Dissatisfied families were those who felt the services they had received had been unhelpful.

More than half of the families were unsatisfied and felt at the end of the study that they would have liked more services. Although professionally referred families were likely to be offered more services, and over longer periods, than the self-referred, almost half felt that they would have liked more services. Over a third of the parents wanting more services had in fact been offered multiple services. Almost two-thirds of the parents who received social work support as a service in its own right wanted more. The following comments from case studies illustrate parents' unmet needs:

He [the social worker] says to me, 'You know, you're in control. You've
got control over your children.' But I haven't. It's easy for him to say that.
You know if you see how my children are with me, or my daughter,
you think it's not for me to blame.

●●●

He [the social worker] told me that I was an intelligent, good mum,
and that I didn't need a social worker. He asked permission to take me
off the computer . . . I feel I've been off-loaded for no reason.'

The desire for more services was not necessarily indicative of negative views
of Social Services:

♦ two-thirds of the parents wanting more services found Social Services
  were sympathetic;

♦ over half of the parents wanting more services found Social Services
  were helpful;

♦ over half of the parents who reported that the provision of social
  services had improved family relationships wanted more services;

♦ almost two-thirds of the parents who reported that the provision of
  social services had helped with child development wanted more
  services;

♦ more than half of the parents who reported that the provision of
  social services had relieved stress wanted more services; and

♦ half of the parents who reported that the provision of social services
  had alleviated a practical problem wanted more services.

Those parents wanting more services were expressing their ongoing confidence in Social Services rather than dissatisfaction with the service provision
already made. A third of the parents in this group had felt at the end of their
tether when they approached Social Services. Case studies serve to illustrate
parents' views of the value of continuing the services they had obtained:

A mother of a 2-year-old had originally been referred to Social Services because she was feeling depressed, and also because she wanted help towards playgroup fees. The fees were provided, and she was also offered counselling as her mother had recently died. She still felt at the end of the study that she would like further therapy, from a psychiatrist rather than a counsellor:

> I think I need a psychiatrist . . . I have no self-confidence to go shopping and when I go out I am panicking about fainting in public.

● ● ●

One parent appreciated that a great deal of good help was being provided to her family, with the result that they felt more confident, had more techniques for dealing with behavioural problems and no longer felt that they were coping alone. However, she still felt that foster care would help and give them all a break.

Table 8.2 shows that in almost all of the cases of intrinsic need the parents wanted more services; whereas in cases of need through social deprivation the parents were less likely to want more services. It has been established that the former generally have more complex needs and required more services, whilst the latter are often satisfied with a single, short-term service, such as a one-off financial payment.

Table 8.2 *The parents' attitude to more services, according to category of need*

Parents' attitude	Category of need					
	Intrinsic	**Parental ill health**	**Family stress**	**Offending behaviour**	**Social deprivation**	**Total**
	n=13	**n=12**	**n=36**	**n=6**	**n=23**	**n=90**
No more services wanted	1	5	19	2	9	36
More services wanted	12	7	17	4	14	54

n=90; cases lost from study=3

Families whose needs had changed or who had found other sources of help

Some parents who had been turned down by Social Services had found support elsewhere as the following case study shows:

● ●

> The mother of a 13-year-old girl had gone to Social Services for money towards clothing for her child. The mother had mental health problems and an alcohol problem, for which she was receiving treatment. She had been turned down by Social Services, but the family seemed to know exactly where to obtain financial help and had successfully tried different sources, such as the Department of Social Security and the YMCA.

● ●

The following comments also illustrate the other sources of support available to parents:

> I 'phoned up before and said: 'Look, can you take her for a while, just for a bit of distance?' But in the end, instead of having a bit of help from them, it's been like, relatives and friends that have sort of had her for a few days until everything has calmed down and then she's come back.

> When I got into this trouble with the bailiffs, when they came around to the house, I thought there was no point 'phoning up Social Services again to help me as they had turned me down last time, and I went to the Citizens' Advice Bureau and the man there was so nice and helpful.

At the end of the study, 12 families who had obtained a short-term service did not feel that they needed any more from Social Services: six were parents of children in need because of family stress; five were parents of children in need because of social deprivation; one was the parent of a child in need through parental ill health.

As shown in Table 8.3, at the end of the study a third of the parents who were not offered services did not feel that they needed them. Half of the cases concerned children in need through family stress, and almost a third were cases of need through social deprivation.

Qualitative analysis of the cases shows that there were a number of reasons why parents no longer wanted services for their children, despite the fact that they had not been offered any service. These included:

♦ inappropriate referrals;

♦ independent solutions; and

♦ transient needs.

Table 8.3 *The parents not offered services, according to category of need*

Parents' attitude	Category of need					
	Intrinsic	**Parental ill health**	**Family stress**	**Offending behaviour**	**Social deprivation**	**Total**
No services wanted	–	1	5	1	3	10
Services wanted	5	–	3	2	9	19
Total	**5**	**1**	**8**	**3**	**12**	**29**

In two cases the referral to Social Services did not come from the parents themselves. In the case study outlined below, services were no longer wanted because the parent had not really wanted them in the first place:

● ●

Referred by her health visitor, the mother of a 7-year-old child and a new-born had post-natal depression. The family were relatively affluent and the mother was in a stable marital relationship. The father had been looking after the family, but Social Services were contacted by the health visitor when there was pressure on the father to return to work. The mother did not really want professional input and had been rather ambivalent about the referral in the first place, saying that she was 'not as bad as some', and that she was still able to look after the child. By the time of second interview her feelings had not changed; she felt that she was even more able to look after the child than on the previous occasion. The family had had no previous contact with Social Services.

● ●

In other cases, needs had proved more transient:

● ●

The mother of a 13-year-old approached Social Services in desperation because of the boy's criminal behaviour: lighting fires and shoplifting. She wanted Social Services to 'do something about his behaviour'. However, the problems of her son were superseded by the arrival of a friend of his older brother, who had left his own family and was subsequently fostered by the mother, in a voluntary arrangement, for a short while. By the end of the study, the friend had gone to live with his father, but the son's problems had subsided in the meantime.

● ●

Other parents said:

> We were going through a sticky patch and it was affecting his school work.
>
> He doesn't seem as bad now. I think he may have been sorted without their help. The police have not been round for a long time.
>
> Things seem to have sorted themselves out.

Some families who were referred to Social Services because they had children in need through family stress did not receive services and yet did not want them at the end of the study. These families had been experiencing crises at the time of referral, but these had been overcome and there was no longer any need for services. One case study serves as an example:

● ●

> The ex-partner of a parent had threatened to report her for neglect if she did as she intended, that is, found an evening job and left the younger children in the care of her 15-year-old daughter. The parent wanted to check her position with Social Services, but before she had a response from them she decided not to take the job anyway. Thus the need for services had disappeared.

● ●

Ongoing problems

At the end of the study, some of the children and their families were still experiencing a range of problems, to a greater or lesser degree. The families' problems at the beginning of the study were such that substantial changes to entrenched problems were unlikely to occur within the time-span of the study, although the provision of family support services did moderate needs and improve coping abilities. The continuing presence of problems suggests that there is a strong case for a diversity of family support provision, from 'one-off' contracts with Social Services to longer-term provision. Matching needs to services is critical in helping families to address and ameliorate their problems.

Family problems

Housing problems still affected almost half of the families. Family health problems, in terms of both physical and mental health, remained prevalent in two-fifths of the cases. Over half of the families still had relationship problems, the majority of which were classified as severe. One-fifth of the family problems stemmed from parent–child relationships and a third from sibling relationships. Partnership/marital problems were present in over two-fifths of the families. Over a third of the families lacked informal support.

Children's problems

Over half of the families still had problems with a specific child. Problems of self-control affected almost a third of the children and aggression over a quarter. Children presented a range of continuing problems, including running away, sleeping and eating disorders, deviant behaviour and enuresis.

Specific problems were not restricted to specific needs categories. Families often had multiple problems, any one of which could become a priority at different times. Multiple problems required time and support to alleviate them, if alleviation actually was a possibility. Some problems within families were likely to require solutions from within the families, not simply solutions imposed from outside the family by agencies such as Social Services. Case studies serve to illustrate such ongoing problems:

● ●

A 10-year-old boy was having difficulty coming to terms with his new stepfather and was reacting violently in the family home. The mother did not feel that enough had been done by Social Services. She felt that the child should go into care. Evidently Social Services disagreed, believing that such action was not in accord with the philosophy of the Children Act.

● ● ●

A 9-year-old child, who was suffering from a school phobia, was viewed by her mother as not having improved. The family had an education welfare officer with whom the child had a difficult relationship. He had referred the family to Social Services, as had the housing department, as the family lived in squalor and poverty. The family had social work support for a few months but there was little change in the situation. The family were being threatened with court action because of school non-attendance.

● ● ●

An 11-year-old boy presented extremely difficult behaviour and was uncontrollable: he would lie, light fires and was very difficult at school. To a large extent the problem had subsided by the end of the study: the child had calmed down and was now a 'different child'. However, the mother expressed concerns about the effect that her rejection had had on him. She described herself as having been revolted by him when he was behaving so badly.

●●●●●●●●●●●●●●●●●●●●●●●●●●●●●●●●●●

The verdict on Social Services

This chapter ends with a general review of the parents' attitudes towards Social Services as an enabling or an inhibiting agency. At the beginning of the study, parents gave their views on their concerns about approaching Social Services. These concerns were reviewed at the end of the study.

Information about Social Services

At the end of the study there was reasonable satisfaction with the level of information available about services. Two-thirds of the parents expressed their views, and of these almost three-quarters felt they were given sufficient information about where to obtain services. At this stage just under half felt that they had experienced no difficulties in accessing Social Services.

The families' concerns over contact with Social Services

At the end of the study the majority of parents felt that the process of obtaining services had not been a negative experience. We revisited some of their concerns to see what their experience had been and if it had changed their views. Four areas of concern were discussed:

- ◆ stigma attached to contact with Social Services;
- ◆ lack of partnership between social workers and parents;
- ◆ children being taken away; and
- ◆ misinterpretation of circumstances.

Stigma

At the end of the study well over three-quarters (84%) of the carers who expressed views did not feel stigmatised by their contact with Social Services, compared to 78% at the beginning of the study. There was, however, some variation across needs categories in terms of fear of stigma. The parents who remained most sensitive about stigma were in the parental ill health category (about one-third). About a quarter to one-fifth of the families in the family stress, intrinsic need and offending behaviour categories were still concerned about stigma. Most interesting is the fact that no parents in the social deprivation category expressed concerns about stigma. Professionally referred parents felt more stigmatised than those who had referred themselves.

Partnership

At the end of the study almost two-thirds of the parents felt that there was a degree of partnership between themselves and Social Services. This represented a small decrease from the beginning of the study, when 83% were relatively optimistic about the likelihood of working in partnership with Social Services. It may be that Social Services have still to develop their ability to ascertain need and/or allocate services, in a way that the parents feel is 'democratic'.

Fears of children being taken away

At the end of the study well over three-quarters (89%) of the parents had no fears that Social Services would take their children away, compared to 68% at the beginning of the study. There was some variation across needs categories in terms of this perception. Parents feared this in:

- ◆ no cases of intrinsic needs;

- ◆ 17% of the cases of need because of parental ill health;

- ◆ 10% of the cases of need through family stress;

- ◆ 20% of the cases of need because of offending behaviour; and

- ◆ 17% of the cases of need because of social deprivation.

There was little difference between professionally and non-professionally/self-referred carers in concerns about the removal of children.

Misinterpretation of circumstances

At the end of the study well over three-quarters of the parents did not feel misjudged by Social Services or fearful that their situation was being misinterpreted, perhaps by social workers reading too much into what they had been told. In this respect, there was no difference to the way parents had felt at the beginning of the study. There was some variation across needs categories in terms of misinterpretation. Parents feared this in:

- 23% of the cases of intrinsic need;

- no cases of need because of parental ill health;

- 20% of the cases of need through family stress;

- no cases of need because of offending behaviour; and

- 6% of the cases of need because of social deprivation.

There was little difference between professionally and non-professionally/ self-referred parents in concerns about misinterpretation of families' situations.

Summary

In cases of parental ill health, more benefits were obtained than had been anticipated; in other needs categories, carers maintained that the benefits had been less than they had anticipated at the beginning of the study.

In terms of different types of benefit, the alleviation of practical problems was exceptional in that the benefits obtained exceeded expectations. Relief of stress was a benefit confirmed in 73% of cases in which it had been anticipated; help with child development in 78%; improvement in family relationships in 41%.

Almost 40% of the children had hoped for the resolution of parental conflict; 27% thought this had occurred to some extent. Nearly half of the children were pleased that Social Services had become involved and were happy with the services offered as well as with the outcome of approaching/referral to Social Services.

Overall, 86% of the parents found Social Services sympathetic and helpful. There were more positive views among parents who received single services; less positive views among parents of children with intrinsic needs, despite their high level of services. Parents of children in need through parental ill health had the most positive views than the average: 91% found Social Services sympathetic.

More than half of the parents (60%) wanted more services. This was possibly indicative of a dependence on Social Services, an appreciation of Social Services or the complexity of the families' problems requiring more/ongoing services. Parents of children in need through social deprivation were less likely to want more services.

It is important to distinguish between the notions of 'unsatisfied' and 'dissatisfied'. Many of the families were unsatisfied in that they would have liked a greater amount of service, but they were not dissatisfied with the quality of the service they had received.

9

Delivering Part III services – social workers and others

The legal and administrative framework that governs social work activity in the area of family support under Part III of the Children Act 1989 is primarily determined by both Sections 17 and 27. These two clauses, taken in conjunction with the relevant schedules and guidance, create a network of services at the centre of which is social work (see DoH 2000a). This means that the challenge for social workers is to work within their own professional and organisational domain at the same time as drawing in the contributions of other agencies in order to support their fundamental role of safeguarding and promoting the welfare of children in need.

In this chapter we look 'first' at the activities of social workers *within* Social Services and then we widen the lens to examine the way social workers work *with other* agencies.

In order to set the context for these two domains of social work activity, it is helpful to summarise the roles and tasks of the social workers with the children and families in the study. These categories were generated from the data.

The main roles and tasks of children's and families' social workers

Co-ordination/case management. This is a widely acknowledged part of social work activity with many social work client groups. It involves assessing, selecting and managing the services thought to be relevant to the needs of a particular family, which may include services provided by other agencies. There will be budgetary and organisational elements in the work.

Direct work with parents/families to safeguard and promote the welfare of children. This is a fundamental part of family support services and may take many forms, including psycho-social casework and the application of various methods of working in family groups.

Direct work with children to promote and safeguard their welfare. Part of this work embraces the duty laid down in the Children Act 1989 to consult children and take their wishes and feelings into account in the decision-making process. It also includes a range of social work methods such as psycho-dynamic and behavioural social work.

Advocacy on behalf of children and families. This covers the tasks involved in enabling children and families to succeed in exercising their rights to services and benefits.

Facilitator of services from other agencies. This is an important part of social work. It involves social workers acting as informed facilitators of other services, either through the means of a formal referral or through providing information about other services.

The activities of the social workers involved in the study fell into five core functions. Table 9.1 shows the distribution of these functions across the five categories of need. It is evident that direct work with parents was the most prevalent activity, closely followed by the case management function. Much less direct work was undertaken with children. Advocacy by the social worker was an activity in 12 cases and was often concerned with ensuring maximum benefits, including finances, to promote the welfare of the child. There was a moderate amount of facilitation of other service delivery that involved the liaison with a range of agencies.

Table 9.1 *Main social work functions, according to category of need*

Social work functions	Category of need*					
	Intrinsic	Parental ill health	Family stress	Offending behaviour	Social deprivation	Total
Co-ordination/case management	7	10	14	4	11	46
Direct work with parents	5	5	27	4	9	50
Direct work with children	2	3	12	1	1	19
Advocacy	3	2	5	1	1	12
Facilitation of other services	5	–	7	–	4	16

* Categories are not mutually exclusive

Social workers and family support *within* Social Services

Many families, right across the range of needs categories, said they had appreciated the help provided by Social Services (see Chapter 8). Benefits the parents felt they had received through the involvement of Social Services included relief of stress, help with child development, the alleviation of practical problems and improved family relationships.

Working in partnership with parents and children

One of the key features of the Children Act 1989 is to work in partnership with parents to promote the welfare of the child. This involves recognising that parents will themselves have needs and will also have ideas as to what they want in order to meet those needs. Their views must be acknowledged as part of the plan to improve the circumstances and quality of life of the child. The Children Act also places on workers a duty to consult children and involve them in decision-making.

Table 9.2 shows that the parents felt they had been active participants in the decision-making in just over half of the cases (50 out of 93). The children's opportunities to participate were even more limited. Only seven of the 41 children interviewed played a part in decision-making in spite of the fact

Table 9.2 *Family involvement in the decision-making process, according to category of need*

Those involved	Category of need					
	Intrinsic	Parental ill health	Family stress	Offending behaviour	Social deprivation	Total
Parent(s)	9	4	21	4	12	50
Child	–	1	4	1	1	7
Extended family	1	1	2	1	1	6
Total	**10**	**6**	**27**	**6**	**14**	**63**

n=50 parents out of a possible 93; 7 children interviewed out of 41; 6 extended families out of a possible 93 that over three-quarters of this subset were over 7. The children who were involved were all in their middle years. The circumstances of their involvement related mainly to cases of short-term accommodation and cases where there were child protection issues. Very few members of extended families were involved in decision-making. Four out of six had a major share in caring for children alongside parents.

Parents were most likely to be involved in decision-making in cases of intrinsic need, need through offending behaviour and family stress. There was little evidence of the participation of other family members, a factor that is important given the increasing trend towards the use of family group conferences, where social workers, families and other professionals will collaborate in decision-making.

On one level, the fact that half of the parents felt they were not active decision-makers in the provision of services is of some concern. On the other hand, the nature of this study is that it was concerned in large degree with the process of access to services, involving one-off interviews with parents or referrals elsewhere. The revelation of little participation suggests that in Social Services there remains a strong service-led 'gatekeeping' function from which parents are, by definition, excluded. At the same time, the motivation for the majority of parents was to obtain services, by whatever means. Therefore, in the parents' eyes, there was far less concern about the absence of what might be called 'a partnership' approach, provided they obtained a service. This issue raises several questions, not least of which is the scarcity of both choice in and availability of services. Remedying these deficits would have a positive impact on increasing the involvement of parents in the decision-making process.

Two cases illustrate the realistic perceptions that parents have:

● ●

One family – young parents with two children, the younger of whom had been diagnosed as having cerebral palsy – had just moved into the area of one of the study authorities. The mother went to Social Services to seek a day-care place for the older child. She said:

To be honest, I was so desperate to get a place for him, I just wanted them to say *yes*. She didn't discuss much about where it would be, but I would have taken anything.

● ● ●

A father of a child who had been excluded from school said:

> Yes, we could have talked a lot about what we wanted but what is the point? We knew from before Social Services has no money, and we were just happy to leave it to them to sort out. After all, they are the experts, aren't they?

● ●

A further way of exploring how far parents and social workers were working in partnership at the beginning of the study was to ask social workers to comment on how far the four dimensions of anticipated benefits matched their own plans for the children and the families. Table 9.3 shows the main outcomes to which parents aspired and the extent to which social workers had included these outcomes in their plans.

Table 9.3 *Congruence between parents' anticipated benefits and social work assessment (number of cases)*

Type of service	Parents' anticipated benefits	Social workers' planned action
Relief of stress	66	52
Help with child development	40	46
Improvement in family relationships	39	29
Alleviation of practical problems	28	31

n=>93; categories are not mutually exclusive

There was a fairly close fit between the views of the social workers and those of the parents. More parents than social workers anticipated relief from stress. From the social workers' comments it seemed likely that they were approaching parental stress from the position of their wider knowledge of the families and were locating individuals within a broad range of problems with which they were familiar. It may well be, therefore, that social workers did not appreciate that some families were more stressed than they appeared to be.

In the initial screening of the families, identification of risk, rather than the impact of risk on the children's development, was the key criterion for accessing services. But at the point of a fuller assessment, social workers shared parents' concerns about their children's development. Parents tended to express these issues in terms of the children's behaviour. This is a positive finding and suggests that social workers are taking seriously the twin aims of safeguarding and promoting the welfare of the child.

More families than social workers anticipated improvements in family relationships. As described in Chapter 8, few families had been able to effect changes in partner relationships over the time of the study. It may well be that using the wider context of their knowledge, the social workers tended to be more realistic about potential change in this area.

The finding that social workers and families shared the agenda of alleviating practical problems supports the conclusion in Chapter 8 that parents were pleased that they were offered practical services which were outside their initial knowledge or experience.

Overall, the parents' expectations and the social workers' planned actions corresponded reasonably closely. Putting together what the parents recounted (see Chapter 8) and the views of social workers (examined in this chapter), it does seem that there is cause for optimism and that the parents and social workers were succeeding in working together.

Social work activity

The parents had anticipated benefits in four main areas. The social workers had a broader agenda for reaching outcomes that would safeguard and promote the children's welfare. A range of social work activity was involved in the achievement of these outcomes, including:

- working to alleviate family hardship;

- addressing the parents' mental health problems;

- addressing the children's behaviour;

- addressing the families' lack of support;

- empowering the parents;

- increasing parenting skills;

- preventing family breakdown;

- relieving stress;

- increasing the children's self-esteem; and

- safeguarding the children's welfare.

Table 9.4 shows the distribution of social work activity across the five categories of need.

Table 9.4 *Social workers' activities to respond to the children's and families' problems*

Target	Category of need					
	Intrinsic	Parental ill health	Family stress	Offending behaviour	Social deprivation	Total
Alleviation of family hardship	3	1	6	1	20	31
Addressing carers' mental health problems	3	4	8	2	6	23
Addressing children's behaviour	9	3	20	5	6	43
Addressing families' lack of support	5	8	12	2	5	32
Empowerment of carers	3	2	10	1	3	19
Increasing parenting skills	4	1	9	1	3	18
Prevention of family breakdown	4	2	7	3	2	18
Relief of stress	5	9	11	3	7	35
Increasing children's self-esteem	1	1	5	1	–	8
Addressing children's welfare	5	3	7	1	6	22
Total	**42**	**34**	**95**	**20**	**58**	**249**

Categories of activities are not mutually exclusive, therefore total activities for 93 children=249

The following provides a detailed examination of the activities shown in Table 9.4 within each category of need and explores the similarities and differences across the categories of need.

Intrinsic need

Cases of intrinsic need involved 14% of the families in the study. Activities in cases of intrinsic need represented 17% of all proposed social work intervention. The most prevalent activity in this category was addressing children's behaviour: This seemed appropriate given the extent to which the children's own behaviour problems had placed them in this category. Attending to the children's behaviour was also supported by action to safeguard the children's welfare, to relieve families from the stress of coping with children's problems and to put in support to augment the families' own coping resources. There was little emphasis on empowering the parents or enhancing the children's self-esteem.

The distribution of social work in this needs group is interesting. While the concentration with children's behaviour – and the recognition of the stress this places on a family – is clearly relevant, it is unlikely that sustained improvement in a child's behaviour will be achieved without helping and strengthening the parents' responses to their children. As shown in Chapter 8, the parents demonstrated their recognition that addressing their own needs was a necessary part of the strategy to help them respond appropriately to their children.

Parental ill health

Cases of parental ill health involved 14% of the families in the study. Activity in cases of parental ill health also represented 14% of all social work intervention. The most likely activities were relief of stress and addressing the families' lack of support. The least likely activities were alleviation of hardship, increasing parenting skills and increasing the children's self esteem.

This multi-faceted strategy to concentrate on supplementing the parents' capabilities would appear to be appropriate in cases where a parent is incapacitated by mental or physical illness. This response recognises the social isolation of many of the families of children in need.

Family stress

Cases of family stress involved 39% of the families in the study. Activities in cases of family stress represented 38% of all proposed social work intervention. The most likely activity was to address the children's behaviour, followed by measures to relieve stress and direct work to empower parents. There was also work to address the families' problems of social isolation and lack of support. Low priority was given to alleviating family hardship and responding to the possibility of family breakdown.

When families were under stress the social work activities focused on addressing the children's behaviour, putting in more support for the families, or putting in measures such as short-term accommodation to relieve their distress. Although there seems to be a multi-faceted approach, there is once again a concentration on addressing children's behaviour. A strategy that looks at the strength of each family member and the contribution each can make to alleviating stress in the family may have a more long-lasting impact.

Offending behaviour

Cases of offending behaviour involved only 6 of the families in the study. Activity in cases of offending behaviour represented 8% of all proposed social work intervention. As might be expected, the most likely intervention for the children in need in this category was that of addressing the children's behaviour, but this was not necessarily done in conjunction with either empowering the parents or increasing their parenting skills. Prevention of family breakdown and relief of stress were also issues in three of the cases of need through offending behaviour. In two of the cases, addressing the carers' mental health problems and the families' lack of support were targets for intervention.

It is difficult to determine any patterns of activity because of the small numbers. There may be a tension here between a welfare and a justice model of response to children's offending behaviour. But the small number of cases and the parental and social work responses to them did not shed any light on the approaches Social Services were taking.

Social deprivation

Cases of social deprivation represented 27% of the families in the study. Activities in cases of social deprivation represented 23% of all proposed social work intervention. The major focus of activity in these cases was the alleviation of hardship. This overshadowed the importance of any other activity in this needs category. This finding raises the whole question about social work and the relief of poverty. Professional and policy debates over the last 30 years have pointed to the disproportionate poverty of families in touch with Social Services as well as the inappropriateness of mistaking poverty as an indication of parental deficits. It would appear that social workers in this study were well aware of this potential minefield. In their judgement, and in the views of families in the study, many of the problems that had led the families to Social Services derived from a lack of adequate material resources rather than from problems of family functioning.

Working with other agencies

The 1989 Children Act has both consolidated and extended the duties and responsibilities of social services departments. In addition, there are new requirements for local authorities, voluntary agencies and other key statutory organisations, particularly health authorities, to work in partnership. Partnership includes:

- ♦ co-operation and collaboration between local authority social services departments and other public sector organisations; and

- ♦ co-operation and collaboration between local authority social services departments and voluntary organisations.

In practice, within social services departments themselves there is also a need for joint working. Many families in the study had multiple needs requiring multi-agency intervention and support. Families were involved with other agencies prior to and independently of approaching or being referred to Social Services.

In examining interagency working, the study was informed by the classification suggested by the Social Services Inspectorate (1995):

♦ **communication:** one agency tells another what it intends to do;

♦ **consultation:** one agency asks another for an opinion, information or advice before finalising plan;

♦ **collaboration:** independent service provision with joint planning and agreement on responsibilities and boundaries;

♦ **bilateral planning:** an overlap in service provision with operational interaction arising out of common planning; and

♦ **joint planning:** different agencies working operationally to the same plan.

The introduction of Children's Services Plans has made it compulsory for Social Services to work with other agencies in the planning and provision of services for children in need. Under Section 27 of the Children Act 1989, responsibility to support children in need lies not only with the Social Services, but also with other local authority and public sector departments such as the education, housing and health services and voluntary agencies.

In the study, interagency working was measured in three ways:

♦ referrals to Social Services from other agencies (already discussed in Chapter 5);

♦ joint decision-making; and

♦ subsequent liaison between Social Services and other agencies.

Joint decision-making

Table 9.5 shows the contribution of various professionals and family members to the decision-making process. It is evident that, within the social work teams, the majority of decisions were more likely to be made jointly than by individual social workers. The team manager appeared to play a key role.

There has been some debate about the role of duty social workers as 'gate-keepers', unhelpfully restricting access to services. However, in this study, duty social workers contributed to decision-making in less than half of the cases; managers were almost always involved. In a small number of cases, involvement extended to other social work teams. This was more likely in cases of need through parental ill health and family stress.

Involvement by health and education service professionals was at a relatively low level (in around one-fifth of the cases). However, this reflected the nature of the problems presented. Education service professionals were more likely to be involved in cases of intrinsic need or need through offending behaviour, which seemed very appropriate. Health service professionals were more likely to be involved in cases of need through family stress, which again was related to the nature of the problems. Health visitors were most likely to be involved in cases of younger children.

Table 9.5 *Professionals' involvement in the decision-making process, according to category of need*

Those involved	Category of need					
	Intrinsic	**Parental ill health**	**Family stress**	**Offending behaviour**	**Social deprivation**	**Total**
Child social work team	13	10	36	5	21	85
Duty social worker	3	6	15	1	16	41
Team manager	12	11	35	6	21	85
Other social worker	–	5	4	1	2	12
Doctor	1	1	4	–	1	7
Health visitor	1	3	5	1	2	12
Teacher	2	–	5	1	–	8
Education welfare officer	5	–	5	2	–	12
Total	**37**	**36**	**109**	**17**	**63**	**262**

Categories are not mutually exclusive, therefore professionals' involvement for 93 families=262

Referrals to other agencies

Although Table 9.1 indicates that social workers saw their main function to be one of referral agent in only 17% of the cases, Table 9.6 shows that almost half of the families in the study were in fact referred on to other agencies. This table provides a context in which to discuss the working between agencies as identified in the study. It is relevant to note that 27 families were referred to the voluntary sector compared with nine, four and eight to other statutory agencies.

Table 9.6 *Referrals to other agencies*

Type of agency	Number of referrals
Voluntary	27
Health	9
Education	4
Housing	8
Total	**45**

Not all families were referred to other agencies; 45 out of 93 were referred

Working with the voluntary sector

Voluntary agency referrals included a number of families for whom Social Services acted as an advocate to obtain funds, for example for heating or for a nursery placement. Other voluntary agencies included family centres and Barnardo's young carers' groups, organisations such as Homestart and schemes that were often local to particular areas. Services such as day care, direct work with children, holiday playschemes, family centres and support groups could be provided:

♦ **directly:** by social services' children and families teams; and

♦ **indirectly:** by voluntary agencies wholly or partly funded by Social Services, such as family centres.

Working with education

The study has shown that referrals from schools or education welfare services are low, despite school often being the place where children's problems first come to the light of professionals. There is a tendency for education services to refer cases to Social Services only where there are child protection concerns.

There is no reason why educational problems should be viewed in isolation from other aspects of children's development. The study suggested that educational problems were being viewed as separate from behavioural problems. It is, of course, possible that education personnel, such as teachers and headteachers, may be more likely to make a referral to the education welfare service in the first instance.

Approximately one-third of the children were experiencing behavioural problems within the school setting, and some were actually truanting or being excluded from school. Just under one-tenth of the children in the study who were of school age had had support from education welfare, independently of the intervention of Social Services. The parents of children who attended special schools spoke more positively about the nature and scope of the support they were given.

Sometimes it seemed as though there was little recognition of the connections between children's health, educational and social problems. Families of children with problems felt under pressure to select one aspect of the multi-faceted problems their children were experiencing in order to present a coherent case for services to a particular agency. This was particularly true in relation to education and health, but it was clear that social workers were sometimes able to see all sides of the problem, as the following case study shows. A mother commented:

> We would get on to health, we would get on to education, it was always somebody else's problem, whereas the social worker said: 'I can see the problems, we will do something about it'. And that, in itself, just the fact that someone was saying yes we will do something meant a lot to me.

Where there was communication between education and social services departments this made a positive difference to parents' perceptions of the help they were receiving:

● ●

> The parent of a child who had behavioural problems at school and at home had a great deal of help, such as a special needs teacher and a behaviour modification worker from the education authority, as well as support from Social Services. The parent commented: 'I think they all talk to each other, actually.'

● ●

Working with health

There was a high level of referrals from health services – mainly from health visitors rather than from general practitioners. Social Services were unlikely to refer cases on to health services if they were not themselves involved. Referrals might well be made to child and family consultation centres (where they were available), with the social worker maintaining a case management role.

In Chapter 4 it was suggested that children and their families suffered a high level of health problems, approximately two-thirds of the parents or children having physical or mental health problems. In spite of this high prevalence of health problems, only one-fifth of the families were receiving support from health services independently of Social Services. These families were receiving help from psychiatrists, community psychiatric nurses, psychologists, health visitors and doctors.

The case for joint funding

The experiences of the children and the families in the study make a strong case for the development of joint funding for health, education and social services. Social workers spent considerable amounts of time presenting cases to their managers and other agencies in order to obtain funding to promote the welfare of children in need. The following two case studies illustrate the hurdles to be overcome:

⬤ ⬤

The mother of a child with Attention-Deficit Hyperactivity Disorder felt that her child's needs would best be met in a school for behaviourally disturbed boys, as he had both educational and social needs. However, no individual authority would take responsibility for the funding. In a situation where Social Services had a local policy that prevented them from offering money towards residential care for children under the age of 12, the child went without the help that was needed.

⬤ ⬤ ⬤

A child with drug-induced psychosis was in inappropriate residential care for months because there was no agreement as to the type of long-term care to be provided, principally because appropriate care was expensive. The parent commented:

> All departments bat off each other. Three months passes and they say: 'We're taking this seriously.' But still nothing has been done. It takes a long time to set meetings up with all those people, and at the end of it, what was it all about – nothing!

⬤ ⬤

Summary

Social workers saw their main tasks to be direct work with parents, case management, direct work with children, referral to other sources of support and monitoring child protection cases.

Decision-making tended to be service-led. The parents participated in decision-making in only half of the cases; and the children in very few cases. Parents were more concerned about obtaining services rather than with the nature of the process.

Social workers rarely made decisions alone. First-line managers were key professionals in decision-making about the children and families to receive services.

There were similarities between the parents' expectations of services and the social workers' planned actions.

The average number of social work activities per child was three, except in cases of social deprivation where it was two. The most likely social work activity was that of addressing children's behaviour; the least likely was increasing children's self-esteem.

There was little evidence of joint decision-making and joint working. Decisions were generally made jointly by the social services team; other professionals were involved in less than a quarter of cases.

10 Implications for policy and practice

In this chapter we review the implications of the study findings for the roles of both social services departments and social workers. This study was commissioned by the previous Tory government, and since 1997, the present Labour government has given a high priority to policy on children and families. This prioritisation is not synonymous with a high profile for social work as such; indeed many major, post-1997, policy developments have primarily involved education services, the criminal justice system, social security and policy on employment. Ironically, the main debates in the context of social services have been around the failure of social services departments in respect of children in care (DoH 1998 and 1999) and of the place of adoption. A review of adoption, headed by the prime minister, was announced in January 2000. Neither of these two policy areas fall directly within the scope of the study reported here; at face value it may even seem that they are located at very different points of the continuum of child-care social work tasks. However, this would be a misunderstanding of the way in which success or failure in one element of the system has implications for the role of other elements. In this sense, family support services represent the foundation stones of any child-care system. The extent to which policy and practice in the realm of family support selects and meets appropriate objectives will have a profound influence on, for example, the reasons for children being 'looked after' or the need to reform adoption services for those who are not able to live with their birth parent(s).

In addition, the emphasis since 1997 has moved from 'family support' to 'parenting services'. The definition of parenting services and the focus of, for example, the work by the National Institute for Family and Parenting are far wider than (only) the children who come within the remit of Section 17 of the Children Act 1989. However, conversely, the 'children in need' within this statutory definition – whose experiences we have studied here – do fall within this new and wider policy focus, as the following quote from the 1998 consultation paper on *Supporting Families* makes clear:

> This paper . . . is not about pressuring people into one type of relationship or forcing them to stay together. Instead it is about the practical support the

Government can provide to help parents do the best they can for their children.

All families face pressure in their everyday life and all families want some measure of support. But a small proportion of families encounter more serious problems and need particular help and assistance. Poverty, poor housing, social exclusion and lack of opportunity are at the root of many serious family problems. (Home Office 1998)

Although we have not lost sight of either the context within which the study was commissioned or the original brief, we have taken the new policy agenda into account in drawing conclusions from our findings as to the future direction of policy and practice.

Given that the focus of our study was on the circumstances, experiences and views of children in need and their families, a number of clear pointers have emerged for the design and delivery of existing and proposed policy in this area.

It is essential to listen to the views of children and parents

As well as being clear about the origin and nature of the problems they were experiencing, parents manifested high levels of concern for the welfare of their children and, at the same time, a determination to access *any* services that they considered would help them with their parenting tasks. They were only potentially deterred by considerations of stigma and fears that they might lose their children. Therefore, it is of paramount importance that the presentation, design and delivery of services and facilities maximise the ease with which families can access services. If the views of the children and the families are taken seriously, then this can help to eliminate unnecessary obstacles to service access, such as cumbersome reception and intake arrangements.

In particular, the task of gaining access to services will, as we have shown, inevitably be harder for parents who may already be under some stress. Therefore, more imaginative ways of providing information and publicity about the services available would enable parents under stress to take account of facilities that they can access through Social Services – one important way of meeting their children's needs. Family centres and GP surgeries can increasingly play a part in facilitating access to Social Services.

Opportunity for access to support over longer as well as shorter periods of time

The study indicated the diverse nature of problems experienced by families who seek help from Social Services under Part III of the Children Act 1989. Some families have problems that are due to short-term crises; others have problems that are both complex and enduring.

Some problems experienced by our respondents demonstrated the importance of relatively time-limited and task-centred support, but in other parental circumstances and categories of need there is a clear requirement for the provision of a longer-term service. It is also necessary that families have the opportunity of deciding for themselves when to opt out of or re-access services. Knowing that this is a possibility was itself seen by parents as a form of support; in the light of 'best value', such user-autonomy combined with service flexibility may well represent an extremely cost-effective mode of service configuration.

The importance of social work support

It was clear that the families in the study viewed social workers very positively and valued their social work skills in responding to family distress by means of a *casework* approach. Casework, contrary to common misperception, includes highly developed skills of assessment, purposeful counselling and acting the role of facilitator and advocate. Without this social work intervention many families were clear that their circumstances would have deteriorated to the point of family breakdown. The role and the contribution of social work should, therefore, represent a central component of current policy initiatives in respect of children, young people and families. It is important that their supportive and developmental functions are recognised as an integral part of the social work task, even where there are issues relating, for example, to child protection or to juvenile offending.

The value of an interagency response

While services such as social work support, which have been traditionally categorised within the remit of family support, were valued highly by users, other less traditionally identified resources, such as recreational and sporting facilities, were seen to make important contributions to the developmental needs and welfare of the children. Professional guidelines in statutory agencies and departments other than social services need to emphasise this significance.

In order for this facilitation to become a reality for families it is clear that there will have to be far more robust and better co-ordinated interagency frameworks between the statutory services such as health, education, the police and social services. Since the study was commissioned Children's Services Plans have been developed, and these are enabling local authorities to be more actively involved in working together. This study confirms the crucial importance of interagency working that is well planned and delivered at all levels.

Other less traditionally recognised resources are also of critical significance to the quality of a child's life. These include transport policies, recreational and sporting facilities and after-school provision for children of working parents. The goal for all statutory agencies and departments other than social services should be an acknowledgement of the need for a 'whole child approach' to developing services, rather than a pre-occupation with the 'part of the child' with whom they are concerned. Social Services has a valuable role to play in facilitating and co-ordinating access for children in need to other services, as well as providing direct Part III services themselves. Social workers should be at the heart of these arrangements.

A differential approach to children of different ages

The study data underlined the severity of family and parenting problems in respect of all age groups as well as the paradoxical deficit of accessible services to address them. More attention and imagination need to be applied to the design and delivery of age-relevant services, as well as to access points that are relevant to parents' responsibilities towards their children throughout the early years, middle childhood and the transition to adolescence. The study reveals a dearth of family support services for children in their middle and teenage years. This is of concern because it means there is very little early intervention to address the problems of this age range, such as mental health or substance abuse. If such problems are not addressed at an early stage, the children and young people in question may find themselves precipitated into care or into juvenile offending systems. There is an urgent need for the development of early intervention mental health services for older children.

There is also a dearth of good community facilities for young people. An emphasis that combines individual interventions with community regeneration would be welcomed. In short, an ecological approach to services that addresses the interface between child, family and community is highly desirable.

Finally, it is important not to neglect the younger age group. Some families in the study were under very considerable stress. The impact of new initiatives aimed at young children, such as Sure Start, may be helpful in this area.

Recognition of the impact of child poverty

Providing family support services is clearly part of a strategy to create optimal life chances for children in need. On their own, such interventions will be wasted unless there is a simultaneous attack on the structural problems that underpin the lives of children in need. Child poverty permeates the families in this study and remains the major factor that obstructs equality of opportunity for the vast majority of children in need.

Bibliography

Alderson, P. (1995) *Listening to Children: Children, Ethics and Social Research*, Barkingside: Barnardo's

Aldgate, J. (1977) *Identification of Factors Influencing Children's Length of Stay in Care*, PhD thesis, University of Edinburgh

Aldgate, J. and Bradley, M. (1999) *Supporting Families Through Short-term Fostering*, London: The Stationery Office

Aldgate, J. and Tunstill, J. (1995) *Making Sense of Section 17: Implementing Services for Children in Need within the Children Act 1989*, London: HMSO

Amin, K. and Oppenheim, C. (1992) *Poverty in Black and White: Deprivation in Ethnic Minorities*, London: Child Poverty Action Group

Audit Commission (1994) *Seen But Not Heard: Co-ordinating Community Health and Social Services for Children in Need*, London: HMSO

Barn, R., Sinclair, R. and Ferdinard, D. (1997) *Acting on Principle: An Examination of Race and Ethnicity in Social Services Provision for Children and Families*, London: British Agencies for Adoption and Fostering

Bebbington, A. and Miles, J. (1989) 'The background of children who enter local authority care', *British Journal of Social Work*, Vol. 19, No. 5, pp. 349–68

Bradshaw, J. (1972) 'The concept of social need', *New Society*, Issue 496, pp. 640–3

Bradshaw, J. (1990) *Child Poverty in the UK*, London: National Children's Bureau

Bradshaw, J., Ditch, J., Holmes, H. and Whiteford, P. (1993) *Support for Children – A Comparison of Arrangements in Fifteen Countries*, Department of Social Security Research Report No. 21, London: HMSO

Brandon, M., Thoburn, J., Lewis, A. and Way, A. (1999) *Safeguarding Children with the Children Act 1989*, London: The Stationery Office

Byng-Hall, J. (1992) 'Grandparents, other relatives, friends and pets', in Bentovim, A., Barnes, G. G. and Cooklin, G. (eds) *Family Therapy, Volume 2*, London: Academic Press

Candapa, M., Ball, J., Cameron, C., Moss, P. and Owen, C. (1995) *Policy into Practice: Day Care Services for Children Under Eight*, London: Thomas Coram Research Unit

Cheetham, J., Fuller, R., McIvor, G. and Petch, A. (1997) *Evaluating Social Work Effectiveness*, Milton Keynes: Open University Press

Cleaver, H. and Freeman, P. (1995) *Parental Perspectives in Cases of Child Abuse*, London: HMSO

Cleaver, H., Unell, I. and Aldgate, J. (1999) *Children's Needs – Parenting Capacity: The Impact of Parental Mental Illness, Problem Alcohol and Drug Use, and Domestic Violence on Children's Development*, London: The Stationery Office

Colton, M., Drury, C. and Williams, M. (1993) *Children in Need: Family Support under the Children Act 1989*, Aldershot: Gower

Compton, B. R. and Galloway, B. (1989) *Social Work Processes*, Belmont CA: Wandsworth

Corrie, M. and Zaklukiewicz, S. (1985) 'Qualitative research and case-study approaches: an introduction', in Heggarty, S. and Evans, P. (eds) *Research and Evaluation Methods in Special Education*, Exeter: NFER/Nelson, pp. 114–39

Department of Health (1991) *Guidance and Regulations, Volume 2: Family Support, Day Care and Educational Provision for Young Children*, London: HMSO

Department of Health (1995) *Child Protection: Messages from Research*, London: HMSO

Department of Health (1998) *Quality Protects Circular: Transforming Children's Services*, Local Authority Circular (LAC(98)28), London: The Stationery Office

Department of Health (1999) *The Goverment's Objectives for Children's Social Services*, London: The Stationery Office

Department of Health (2000a) *The Children Act Now: Messages from Research*, London: The Stationery Office

Department of Health (2000b) *Framework for the Assessment of Children in Need and Their Families*, London: The Stationery Office

Department of Health and Social Security (1985) *Social Work Decisions in Child Care*, London: HMSO

Freeman, M. D. A. (1992) *Children, Their Families and the Law*, Basingstoke: Macmillan

Freeman, P. and Hunt, J. (1998) *Parental Perspectives on Care Proceedings*, London: The Stationery Office

Gibbons, J. (1990) *Family Support and Prevention: Studies in Local Areas*, London: HMSO

Gibbons, J. (ed.) (1992) *The Children Act 1989 and Family Support – Principles into Practice*, London: HMSO

Gibbons, J., Thorpe, S. and Wilkinson, P. (1990) *Family Support and Prevention: Studies in Local Areas*, London: HMSO

Glass, N. (1999) 'Sure Start: the development of an early intervention programme for young children in the United Kingdom', *Children and Society*, Vol. 13, pp. 257–64

Gray, P. G. and Parr, E. A. (1957) *Children in Care and the Recruitment of Foster Parents*, Social Survey Paper 249, London: HMSO

Hardiker, P., Exton, K. and Barker, M. (1991) 'The social policy context of prevention in child care', *British Journal of Social Work*, Vol. 21, No. 4, pp. 341–59

Hearn, B. (1995) *Child and Family Support and Protection: A Practical Approach*, London: National Children's Bureau

Hickman, A. and Barnes, J. (1993) 'Findings from SSI's national survey on Children's Services Plans', paper given at the Social Services Research Group Workshop (unpublished), 26 November 1993

Holman, B. (1988) *Putting Families First*, Basingstoke: Macmillan

Home Office (1998) *Supporting Families : A Consultation Document,* London: The
    Stationery Office

James, A. (1993) *Childhood Identities, Self and Social Relationships in the Experience of
    the Child,* Edinburgh: Edinburgh University Press

Kellmer Pringle, M. (1975) *The Needs of Children,* London: Hutchinson

Knapp, M. (1984) *The Economics of Social Care,* London: Macmillan

Kumar, V. (1993) *Poverty and Inequality in the UK: The Effects on Children,* London:
    National Children's Bureau

Langdon, M. (1998) *Welfare, Needs, Rights and Risks,* London: Open University
    Press/Routledge

Levitt, J. L., Guacci-Franco, N. and Levitt, J. (1993) 'Convoys of support in
    childhood and early adolescence: structure and function', *Developmental
    Psychology,* Vol. 29, No. 5, pp. 222–31

Little, M. and Gibbons, J. (1993) 'Predicting the rate of children on the Child
    Protection Register', *Research, Policy and Planning,* Vol. 3, No. 2, pp. 15–18

Lloyd, C. (1993) *Rowntree Project – Young People in Difficulties: An Interagency
    Project,* York: Joseph Rowntree Foundation

Mahon, A., Glendinning, C., Clarke, K. and Craig, G. (1996) 'Researching
    children: methods and ethics', *Children and Society,* Vol. 10, pp. 145–54

Maslow, A. (1970) *Motivation and Personality,* New York: Harper and Row

Middleton, S., Ashworth, K. and Walker, R. (1994) *Family Fortunes,* London:
    Child Poverty Action Group

Morrow, V. and Richards, M. (1996) 'The ethics of social research with children: an
    overview', *Children and Society,* Vol. 10, No. 2, pp. 90–105

Packman, J. (1968) *Child Care – Needs and Numbers,* London: Allen and Unwin

Packman, J. (1975) *The Child's Generation,* Oxford: Basil Blackwell

Packman, J.(1986) *Who Needs Care? Social Work Decisions about Children,* Oxford:
    Basil Blackwell

Packman, J. and Hall, C. (1998) *From Care to Accommodation,* London: The
    Stationery Office

Parker, R. (1990) *Away From Home,* Barkingside: Barnardo's

Parker, R. A., Ward, H., Jackson, S., Aldgate, J. and Wedge, P. (eds) (1991)
    Looking After Children: Assessing Outcomes in Child Care, London: HMSO

Petrie, P., Poland, J. and Wayne, S. (1992) *Play and Care Out of School,* London:
    Thomas Coram Research Unit

Robbins, D. (1990) *Putting It in Writing: A Review of English Local Authorities Child
    Care Policy Statements,* London: HMSO

Robbins, D. (1993) *Community Care: Findings from Department of Health Funded
    Research Results 1988–1992,* London: HMSO

Rose, W. (1992) 'Foreword', in Gibbons, J. (ed.) *The Children Act 1989 and Family
    Support – Principles into Practice,* London: HMSO, pp. ix–xiii

Rutter, M. (1970) 'Sex differences in children's responses to family stress', in
    Anillary, E. J. and Kaupernick O. (eds) *The Child and His Family,* New York:
    Wiley, pp. 58–79

Rutter, M. (1985) 'Family and school influences on behavioural development', *Journal of Child Psychology and Psychiatry*, Vol. 26, No. 3, pp. 349–68

Sharland, E., Seal, H., Croucher, M., Aldgate, J. and Jones D. (1996) *Professional Intervention in Child Sexual Abuse Cases*, London: HMSO

Sinclair, R. and Carr-Hill, R. (1997) *The Categorisation of Children in Need*, London: National Children's Bureau

Skinner, A., Platts, H. and Hill, B. (1983) *Disaffection from School: Issues and Interagency Responses. An Annotated Bibliography and Literature Review*, Leicester: National Youth Agency

Smith, P. and Grimshaw, R. (1989) 'Breaking down the barriers between disciplines', *Social Work Today*, 9 November, pp. 24–9

Smith, T. (1992) *Family Centres and Bringing up Young Children*, London: Children's Society/HMSO

Social Services Inspectorate (1992), *Capitalising Upon the Act*, London: HMSO

Social Services Inspectorate (1995) *Report on the Analysis of a Sample of English Children's Service Plans 1993/4*, London: HMSO

Social Services Inspectorate (1997) *Responding to Families in Need: Inspection of Assessment, Planning and Decision-Making in Family Support Services*, London: HMSO

Social Services Inspectorate (1999) *Getting Family Support Right: Inspection of the Delivery of Family Support Services*, London: The Stationery Office

Stace, S. and Tunstill, J. (1990) *On Different Tracks: The Inconsistencies Between the Children Act and the NHS Community Care Act*, London: Voluntary Organisations for Personal Social Services

Statham, J. (1994) *Young Children in Wales: An Evaluation of the Children Act 1989 for Day Care Services*, London: Thomas Coram Research Unit

Thoburn, J., Lewis, A. and Shemmings, D. (1993) *Family Participation in Child Protection: A Report for the Department of Health*, Norwich: University of East Anglia

Thoburn, J., Wilding, J. and Watson, J. (2000) *Family Support in Cases of Emotional Maltreatment and Neglect*, London: The Stationery Office

Tunstill, J. and Ozolins, R. (1994) *Voluntary Child Care Organisations After the 1989 Children Act*, Norwich: University of East Anglia/National Council of Voluntary Child Care Organisations

Utting, D., Bright, J. and Henricson, C. (1993) *Crime and the Family: Improving Child-rearing and Preventing Delinquency*, London: Family Policy Studies Centre

Ward, H. (ed.) (1995) *Looking After Children: Research into Practice*, London: HMSO

Index

Index by Mary Norris